HOW TO DRAW TREES

BY GREGORY BROWN

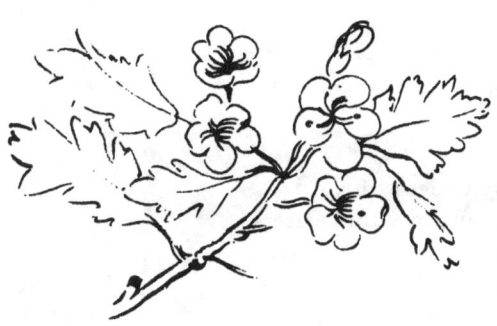

COACHWHIP PUBLICATIONS

Greenville, Ohio

How to Draw Trees, by Gregory Brown
Copyright © 2013 Coachwhip Publications
No claims made on public domain material.
First published 1943.
Front cover: Cherry tree © Sherri Jackson

ISBN 1-61646-194-2
ISBN-13 978-1-61646-194-2

CoachwhipBooks.com

CONTENTS

INTRODUCTION

Most of us love trees. They are our friends in many ways. Some give us fruit and blossom, others wood with which to make a variety of things, but the aspect that appeals to most of us is their beauty all the year round. The countryside is enriched by them and the bareness of the streets is softened by their restful greens.

In this little book, however, we are concerned with the appearance of trees and how best to set about drawing them. Before you start, I think it will help you if I point out a few rather important things.

When a tree is in full leaf, the skeleton, so to speak, that is, the trunk and branches, is still there underneath. The successful drawing of trees depends very much on bearing in mind all the time that the shape of the foliage is relative to the branching. It is rather like drawing a human being fully dressed. If you do not take into account the body inside the clothes, your drawing will not look right.

Another point to notice is the way the branches grow out of each other and out of the trunk, or bole, and are not just stuck awkwardly into each other. If you take care to notice this, you will the more easily get the effect of grace and that wonderful flow of line which is so typical of trees, particularly as seen in winter.

One thing more. Though a tree is made up of millions of leaves, which are very baffling to the beginner, if you look carefully you will find that they form themselves into masses or groups according to how the branches grow. In certain lights these groups can be clearly seen and if drawn properly will give the effect of depth as well as width. How to show all these things in your drawing I shall try to explain in the rest of this book.

There are, of course, many kinds of trees, each having a distinct character of its own and much pleasure can be gained by learning to recognise them. You will also get to understand them better, which will be a great help to you when you start your drawing, for example.

The chief characteristic of the Oak is strength and ruggedness, so noticeable in the massive roots spreading out above the ground. The roots go very deep, so the Oak is rarely uprooted by gales or storms. You will notice that its height is less than the width. The Oak is late in " breaking " yet usually earlier than the Ash. It is often referred to as the King of trees and will live to well over a thousand years.

In contrast to the Oak is the Horse Chestnut. It was introduced into England about the middle of the sixteenth century. In winter it is easily recognised by its very large buds, growing at the ends of heavy branches. In May, it is even more easily recognised, as it is the only large tree common to England that bears flowers of any considerable size. When in full leaf, the Chestnut has a symmetry not found in the Oak. Rather like an inverted pudding-basin in shape it spreads its dense foliage often to within a few feet of the ground. You remember the song, " Under the Spreading Chestnut Tree." By reason of its pudding-basin outline, the Chestnut is not so interesting to draw in its entirety as many other trees. The leaves and branches, however, are particularly beautiful and can be used with great advantage in the foreground of a picture.

Then there is the Silver Birch and although it looks rather like a dainty lady, it is one of the hardiest of trees. The silver bark with its horizontal dark markings, makes it very easy to recognise at any time of the year, and it is decorated with those jolly catkins in the spring. So you see we have the Beech tall, aloof and austere, the Ash more graceful with an air of good-breeding and poise. Then the Horse Chestnut portly and smug, whilst the Silver Birch is a sort of fairy of the forest. The Oak stands amongst them all, bound up with our traditions, unassailable in the majesty of its strength.

In the autumn the leaves of many trees change their colour, ranging from pale yellow, like the Silver Birch, to a rich brown in the Beech. The Copper Beech is, of course, quite distinct for its leaves are of a dark copper colour all through the summer. The Beech and the Oak retain a few dead leaves all through the winter, whilst the leaves of the Ash fall early and have no gay autumn colouring. The Ash, like the Beech and the Oak, is native to English soil and is one of the most beautifully shaped trees you can find. In winter it can be easily singled out by its characteristic branching.

These are some features of a few beautiful trees by which you may come to know them. I have not space to tell you about all the familiar trees, but a little observation on your part will soon get you acquainted with those characteristics that make one tree distinct from another. I feel sure that you will never regret studying them closely.

Life is apt to bring many disappointments and if we are inclined to feel all else has failed us, the trees and grass and flowers of the field always offer refreshment and remind us that the world of nature has still much beauty with which to gladden our hearts.

MATERIALS

I am sure you have often been told that only a bad workman complains of his tools. This is only half the truth, for it is fairly certain that a good workman cannot do his best by using bad tools·

So here is your equipment.

1. Sketch-Book. I have found the Educational Drawing Block, containing Cartridge drawing paper most satisfactory. It can be bought from most artist's colourmen. Although called a " block " it is actually a book, and has a stout cardboard back.

2. Eraser. Though it is better not to rub out, it is sometimes necessary ; a medium-sized piece of soft eraser is what you want.

3. Pencils. A good pencil is never an extravagance.

There is a good selection of pencils, such as, Venus, Royal Sovereign, Koh-i-Noor and Mars. For all round usefulness I recommend a B. An H.B. is useful for some kinds of foliage, and for trunks or branches a 2B is about right. In drawing a complete landscape I use pencils ranging from H to 5B, but that is not necessary when drawing a single tree or group of trees. For your purpose I think pencil is best, though crayons such as BBB, Wolff's Carbon drawing pencil and Hardmuths Koh-i-Noor Polycolor No. 60 black, are very nice to draw with.

The drawings in this book are made with a black crayon pencil largely to facilitate reproduction.

4. Stool. As it is not always possible to find a convenient tree stump, you will be wise to take a stool. Quite a cheap " camp " stool with a webbing seat will do nicely. Don't try to draw standing up as it is difficult to have proper control over your pencil.

PLATE I. STUDY OF BRANCHES

In the first plate I have tried to show the kind of line which I think best for drawing branches and trunks. You will notice that the lines are long and continuous, not made up of short sketchy marks. The sinuous growth, particularly of branches, is more easily expressed by long flowing lines. First of all you should practice making long waving lines close together, tapering towards the ends, like branches do. When you can do this fluently I am sure it will not be difficult for you to draw a long curved line without taking your pencil off the paper. Later on you will be able to put some expression into the line, making part thin and part thick. By so doing it is possible to suggest how a branch twists about, not merely on the same plane as your eyes but in directions that are not parallel to your eyes. When you feel you have gained enough confidence, you can start to draw from the actual tree. Don't be nervous or approach it as if it were a labour. Enjoy it, and whilst taking due care, face it with a spirit of abandon. Otherwise your drawing will look tired and you will fail to capture the " living " quality of the tree. Now you are sitting before your tree and will be sharpening your pencil. Leave a fair length of lead, not a short stubby piece, otherwise your line will be clumsy. Moreover you will be able to keep on drawing for quite a long time without having to stop to re-sharpen it. Don't start to draw straight away but sit quietly and have a good look at your subject. Try to get the general structure fixed well in your mind, and if you do this your drawing will be made with more sureness of touch. Lastly avoid using your eraser as much as possible.

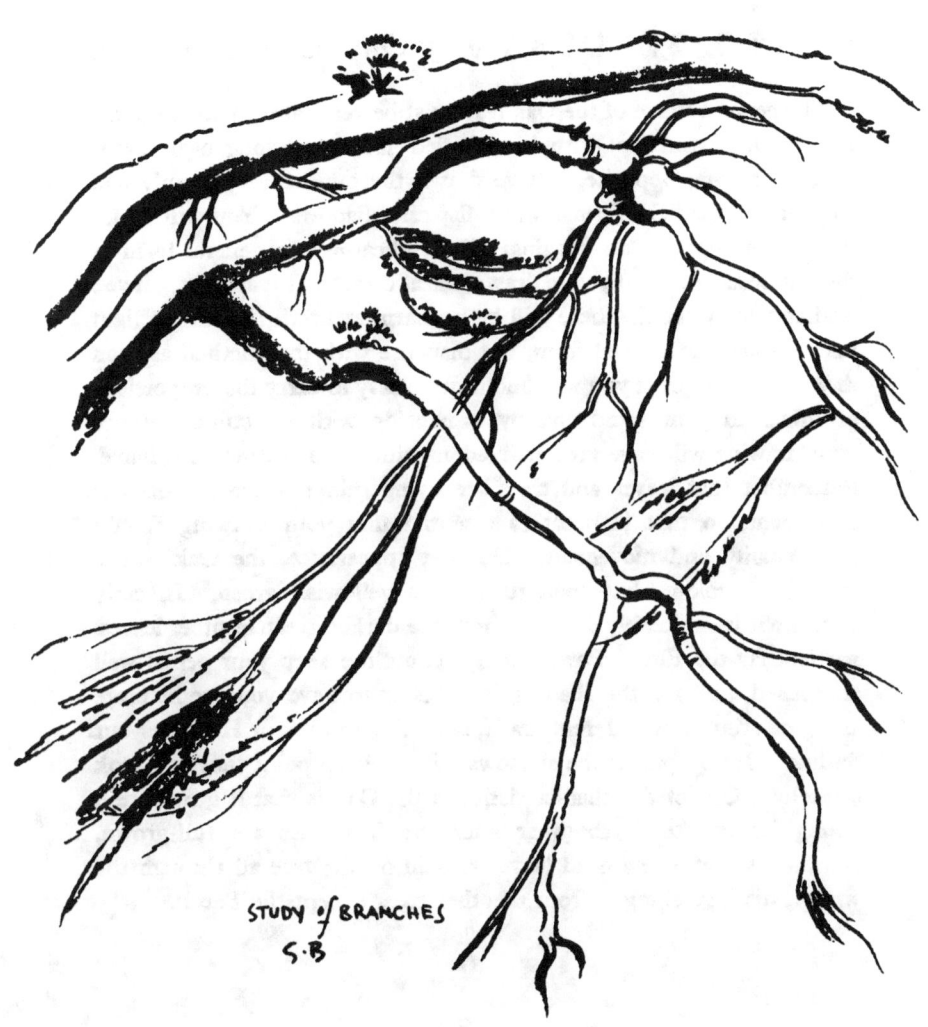

STUDY of BRANCHES
S·B

PLATE 2. LEAVES OF OAK TREE

The general shape of the Oak leaf must be very familiar to everyone. It is quite distinctive, with its rounded lobes and long oval shape. In the drawing opposite, I have drawn the outline very simply and have emphasised the formation by flat cast shadows. You will notice that I have not put an imaginary line indicating the general form of the leaf because I want you to draw the leaf directly as it appears. If you find this too difficult, there will be no harm at first in putting a light line to show the general form, but dispense with this method as soon as you can. In time you will find it quite easy to carry the proportions of things in your mind and by dispensing with structural outlines your drawing will have greater freedom, similar to writing your name. Remember that leaves and trees are living things, often in constant movement, so that it becomes essential that your drawing should have vitality and movement. On first appearance, the Oak leaf is reddish in colour, but soon turns to a yellowish green. In early summer it is noticeably different from the darker green of other leaves, particularly the Elm. For drawing the outline keep your pencil well sharpened, and for the shading it is better to have your point more blunt or even use a different grade, say a 2B, and a B or H.B. for your outline. If you put in the shadows with a sharp point they will look scratchy. One of the characteristics of the Oak is that it grows fresh young leaves late in the year after the first ones are full-grown. Another is that a few dead leaves remain on the tree all through the winter, distinguishing it from all other trees except the Beech.

LEAVES
of OAK TREE

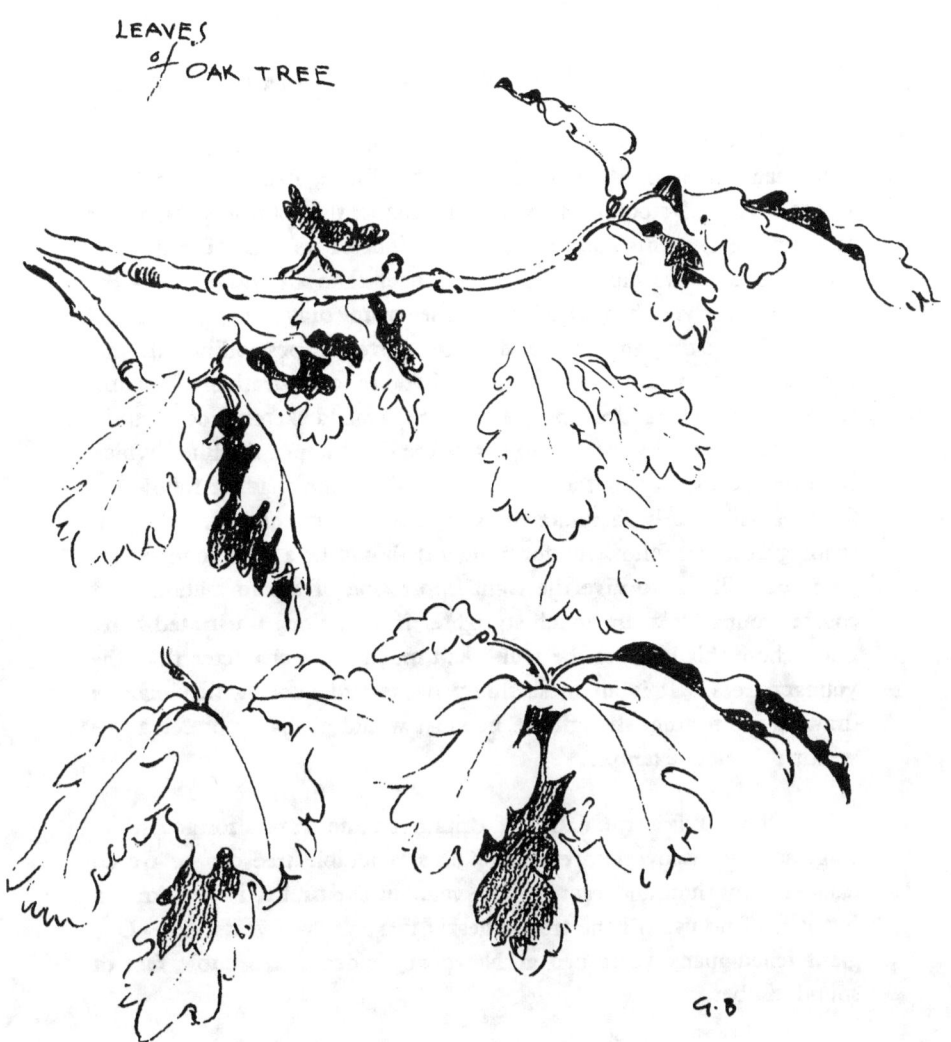

G·B

PLATE 3. TRUNK OF OAK TREE

How very sturdy and strong the trunk of the Oak appears by contrast with many other trees, such as the Silver Birch, Ash or Stone Pine. It has a rugged stockiness, which so eloquently expresses its power to resist the elements and to carry the weight of its massive branches. As the Oak grows old—and it lives longer than any other tree—the trunk becomes very knarled as you will see by my drawing. This makes it very interesting to draw and it gives greater possibilities in this direction than the trunks of trees that are comparatively smooth. On either side of the drawing you will see detailed sketches of portions of the trunk, and I want you to notice the direction of the lines, which indicate the fissures of the bark. By making the shading follow the form, it will greatly facilitate the suggestion of its contour. If your shading does not follow the form, then it should be a solid tone, other-wise you will fail to give the right impression of the formation. Of course, young Oaks are much straighter than the one illustrated here, but I chose this because the trunk had much more character than the younger trees. It is all these funny twists and knots which make a drawing interesting, though the botanist would probably prefer a less weather beaten example.

That the Oak is a true native of Britain is quite certain for according to geological discoveries, remains of this venerable tree can be traced back seventy thousand years. The value of the timber is well-known but it is of no use till the tree is nearly two hundred years old. One giant felled many years ago at Newport yielded 2,426 cubic feet of sound timber.

12

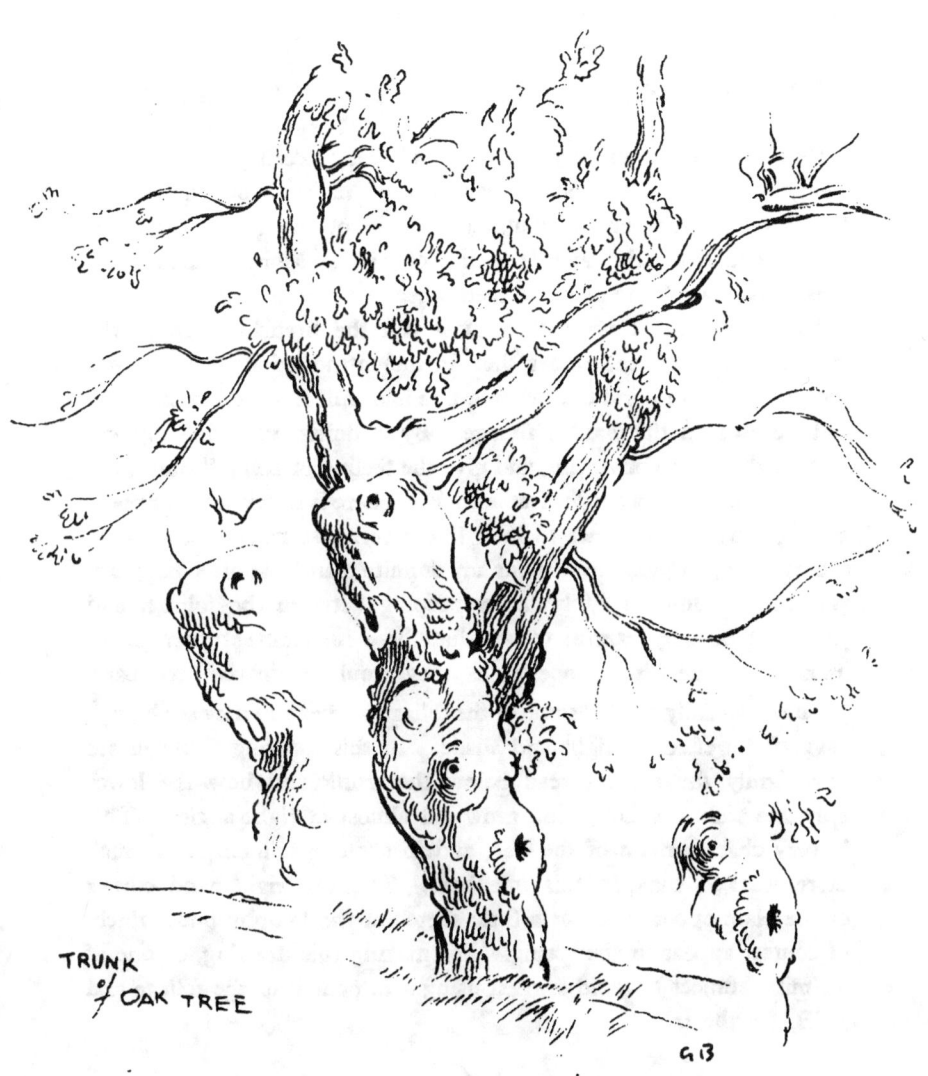

TRUNK
of OAK TREE

G B

PLATE 4. OAK TREE IN LEAF

Here we have a more or less typical Oak. Perhaps it is rather taller, in relation to its height, than most of its kind, but here again I selected it from amongst others because of the good shape and proportion, from the artist's point of view. More branches are shown than would actually be seen when the tree is in full leaf, the reason being that I wanted to show you the branching under the foliage. You will remember that in the introduction I urged you always to keep in mind that when a tree is in full leaf the branches are still there under the mass of foliage. By so doing, your drawing will look all the more convincing and give the feeling of being " built up " and constructed on a proper framework. There is always the danger of getting a tree in summer to look like a formless mass of leaves, as if they were just piled up without any definite plan. As often happens, you do get glimpses of branches peeping between the foliage, and you must be very careful to see that these intermittent portions of branches connect up properly, as they would were the tree bare.

I have partially shaded some of the foliage so that you may see how to suggest the effect of light and shade. In this drawing you will see how firmly the roots spread below the trunk and how the lower branches start low down and grow out almost at right angles. This is very characteristic of the Oak, and in some specimens it is much more marked than in this one here. The top right-hand corner of the plate opposite shows a little sketch of the knobby buds which, of course, appear in the spring. For making this drawing, or one of a similar subject I would suggest using a B. pencil for the foliage and a 2B. for the trunk.

14

OAK TREE
in
LEAF

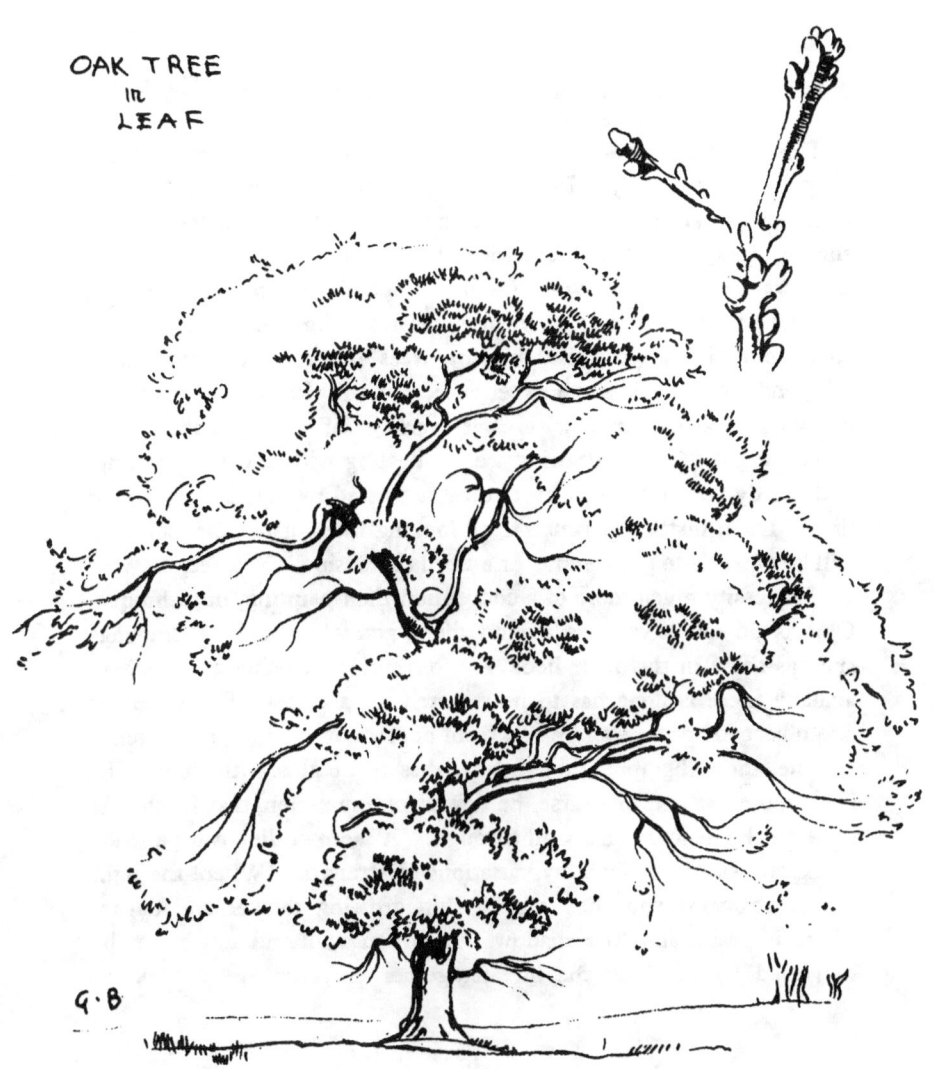

G·B

PLATE 5.   ELM TREE IN FULL LEAF

This plate is to show how to draw the masses of foliage in the simplest possible way. In this manner you will accustom yourself to looking first of all at the big shapes of light and shadow, which should always be the foundation for more detailed work. The shadows are put in here with straight lines with no attempt to suggest leaves, so as to emphasise the relative masses of light and dark without confusion. If you practise drawing trees for a bit in this simple way, and have gained some experience, you will then be able to break up your drawing into a greater variety of tones, and planes. Never forget that it is drawing we are dealing with and not painting, and mostly your tones will have to be suggested by the variety of your line.   Then, instead of your sketch looking like cut-out cardboard, it will be possible to get volume, or a third dimension. You see, drawing is of necessity much more of a convention than painting, in technique. Objects do not have lines around them, and when making drawings such as these in this little book, the convention of using a line where actually there is none has to be resorted to.   The painter separates one object, or part of an object, from another by making a difference in tone, the calligraphic draughtsman has to do this with lines. The line used must not, of course, be devoid of expression, that is, not the same thickness and density all through.   A mere outline can be made to explain the inner form by variations of strength. Where the light strikes strongest, your line can be thin growing thicker and darker where it passes into the shadow. Also you will find much can be suggested by breaking the line altogether in places.

16

ELM TREE
IN
FULL LEAF

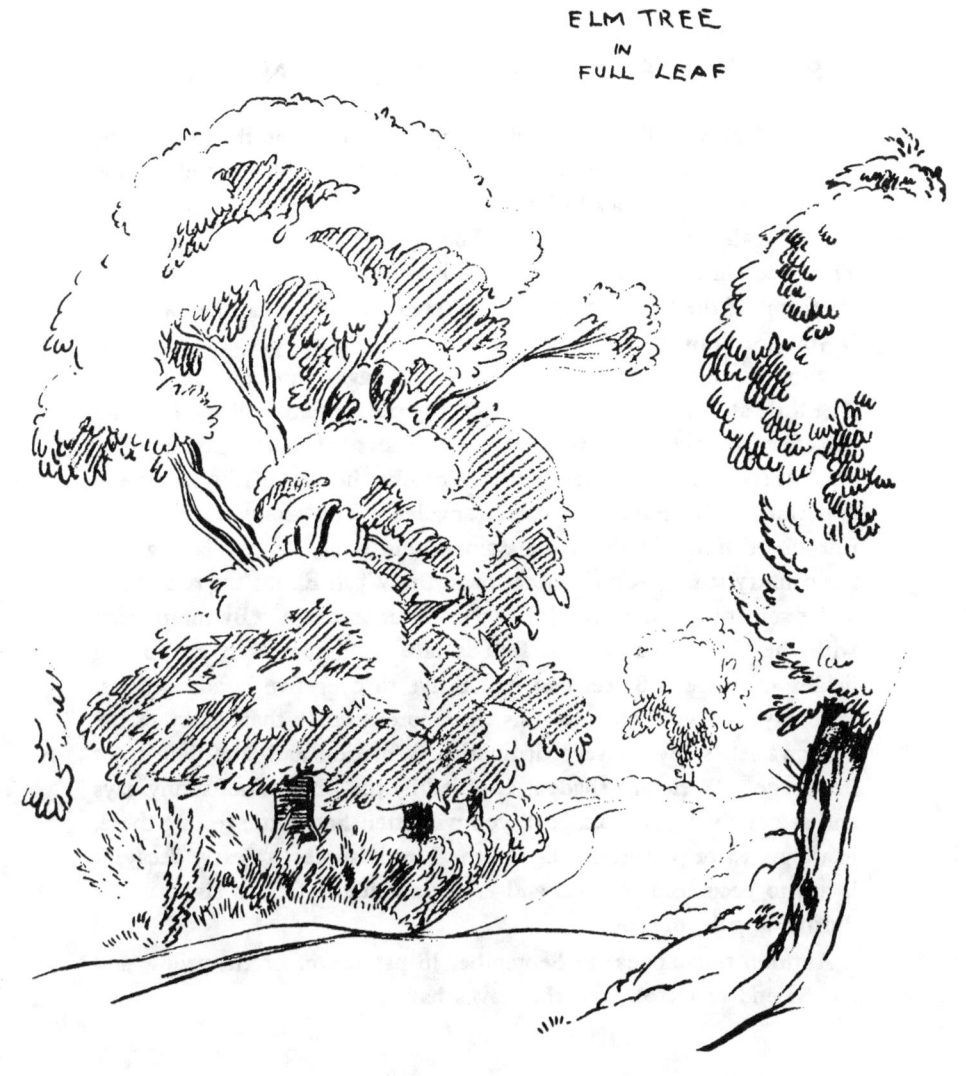

PLATE 6   ELM TREE IN LEAF

Here I have still kept to two simple planes ;   at the same time
I have given a suggestion of masses of leaves, by the method of putting
in the shadows.   Instead of shading them across with straight lines,
I have made a succession of little hooks, something like the letter U.
This group of Elms was drawn when there was a slight wind, so you see
the forms of the foliage are slightly altered from their normal position.
If you are drawing in the wind, a piece of elastic placed across the
bottom of your sketch-book will keep the pages from blowing about.
The little sketches at the top show clearly the formation of the Elm and
the effect it gives in strong sunshine.   These are of the Common, or
small leaved Elm, and though it is very like the Wych Elm in general
appearance, the leaves are much smaller.   The Common Elm was
introduced into Britain by the Romans and is now a familiar sight in
the country lanes.   On the other hand the Wych Elm is the real native
and is sometimes called Wych Hazel or Mountain Elm.   By comparison
with the Oak (Plate 4), the Elm is taller and narrower, reaching a
height of some 120 feet and it will live to over five hundred years.
Probably you will recognise this tree more quickly than many of the
other varieties, by its very distinctive formation and the density of
its foliage.   Welcome shade is afforded by the Elm on hot sunny days
and as grass will grow under it, you will often find cattle resting there,
in the midst of pasture-land.   As the Elm is subject to early decay, it
is apt to become dangerous and is not a suitable tree to stand under
during a gale of wind.

Autumn tints appear in September in patches of bright yellow and
by the end of October all the leaves have gone.

ELM TREE
IN
FULL LEAF

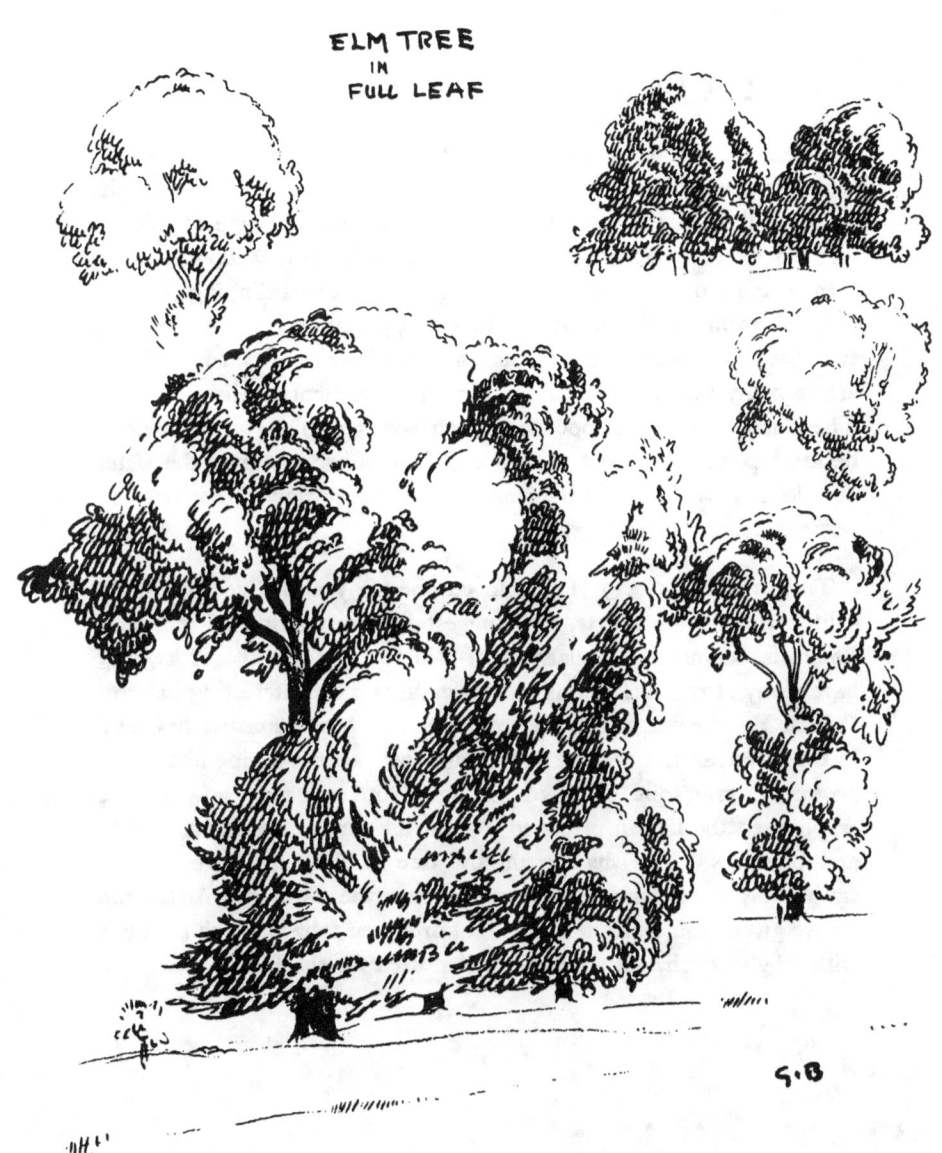

G·B

PLATE 7. WILLOW TREES

When you are using your cricket bat, you may not always realise that it is made from the wood of the Willow Tree. It is the straight boled Willow that is used for this purpose, but the type of Willow which I expect you will have in mind is the Pollard Willow so often seen hanging over the pond with its graceful leaves dipping into the water. From the slender shoots that spring from the top of the bole, such useful articles as lobster-pots and hand-baskets are made. There are so many varieties of Willow that I cannot mention them all here. The illustration on the opposite page shows a group of Pollard Willows beside a pond. I expect you have often climbed out over the water on a leaning Willow, and the wonder is that they stay in that position without falling altogether.

This drawing is very largely in outline, as you will see, with just a little shading on the trunks, suggesting the marking of the bark. Botanists deplore the pollarding of Willows, but for the artist they have many attractions in this state forming a most interesting pattern. Pollard Hornbeams are rather the same, and how fantastic they look in the forest, in the evening light, with their arms twisting about like posturing, grotesque old men. I want you to notice how I have emphasised the line in places to suggest the inner form of the trunks and branches The shading on the tree to the right gives a very simple way of explaining the form between the outlines. At the top I have given an indication of the light drooping foliage which is drawn with a light touch, not so heavy as that used for the Elm.

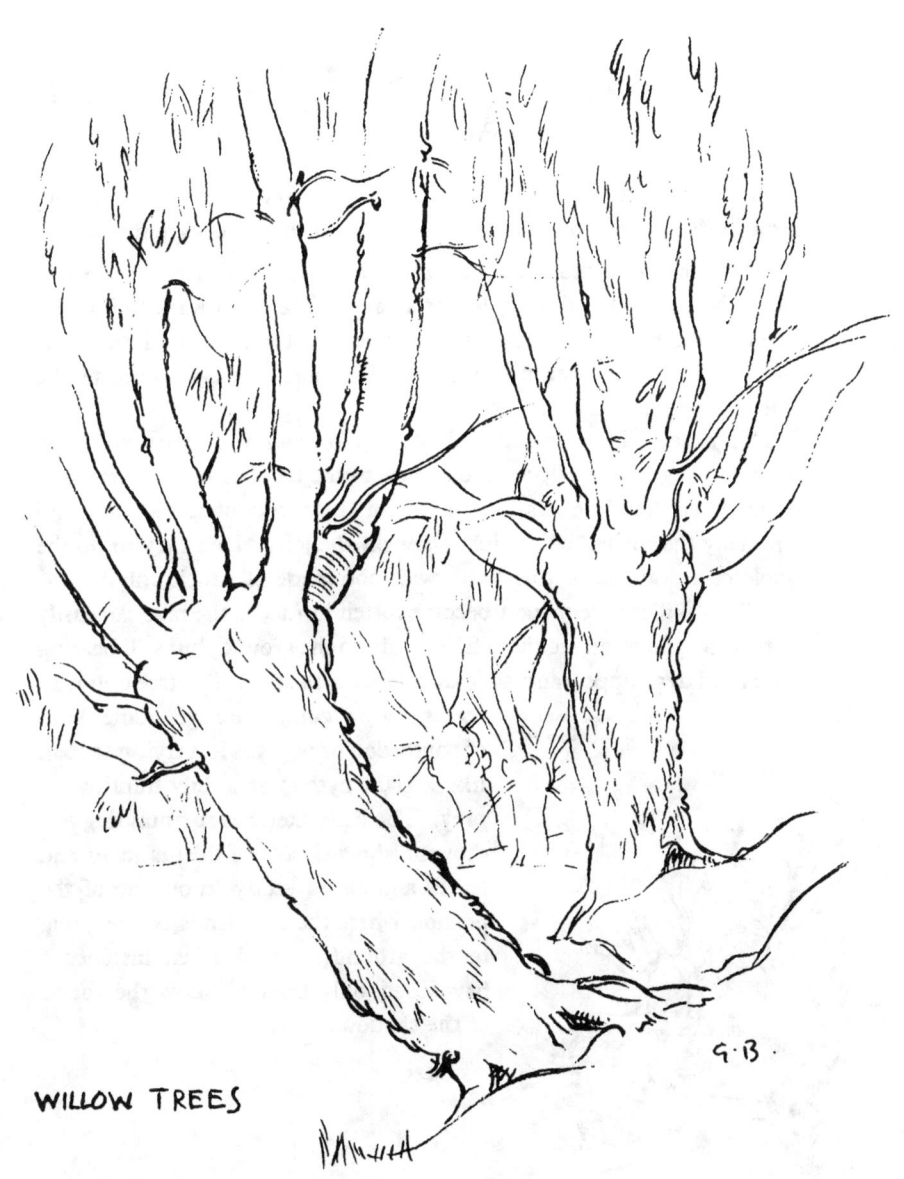

WILLOW TREES

PLATES 8 & 9. WILLOW TREES IN LEAF, AND FALLEN WILLOW

In this row of Willows in leaf you can see the pliable shoots growing from the top of the trunks, from which baskets are made.

There are more branches showing than would ordinarily be visible when the tree is in full leaf, but as I said before, I do want to impress upon you the value of keeping in mind the framework of the tree. Here again I have used a thin line and a light touch, to indicate the delicate airy quality of the foliage.

This time, I have introduced some foreground, so that you may see how to give the effect of distance to the trees in the background. A much heavier line has been used for the banks of the stream and especially the rushes which just show on the left. Don't try to do the whole of a drawing of this kind, with one grade of pencil only.

Pollard Willows very soon become rotten inside, as the rain can easily seep in. So you often see them fallen right to the ground, but still bearing leaves and to all appearances looking very much alive. The tree opposite

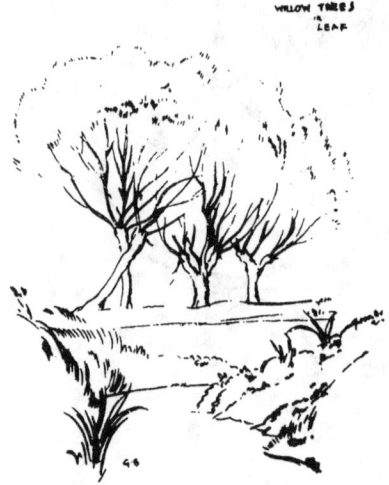

seems to be going through some kind of contortion or perhaps it is trying to look like a giant python stealthily hunting its prey. The little sketches surrounding this drawing show details of the branches and leaves and also a study in outline of the portion where the tree bends before going to the ground. In this last instance I have used only lines to show the forms of the shadows.

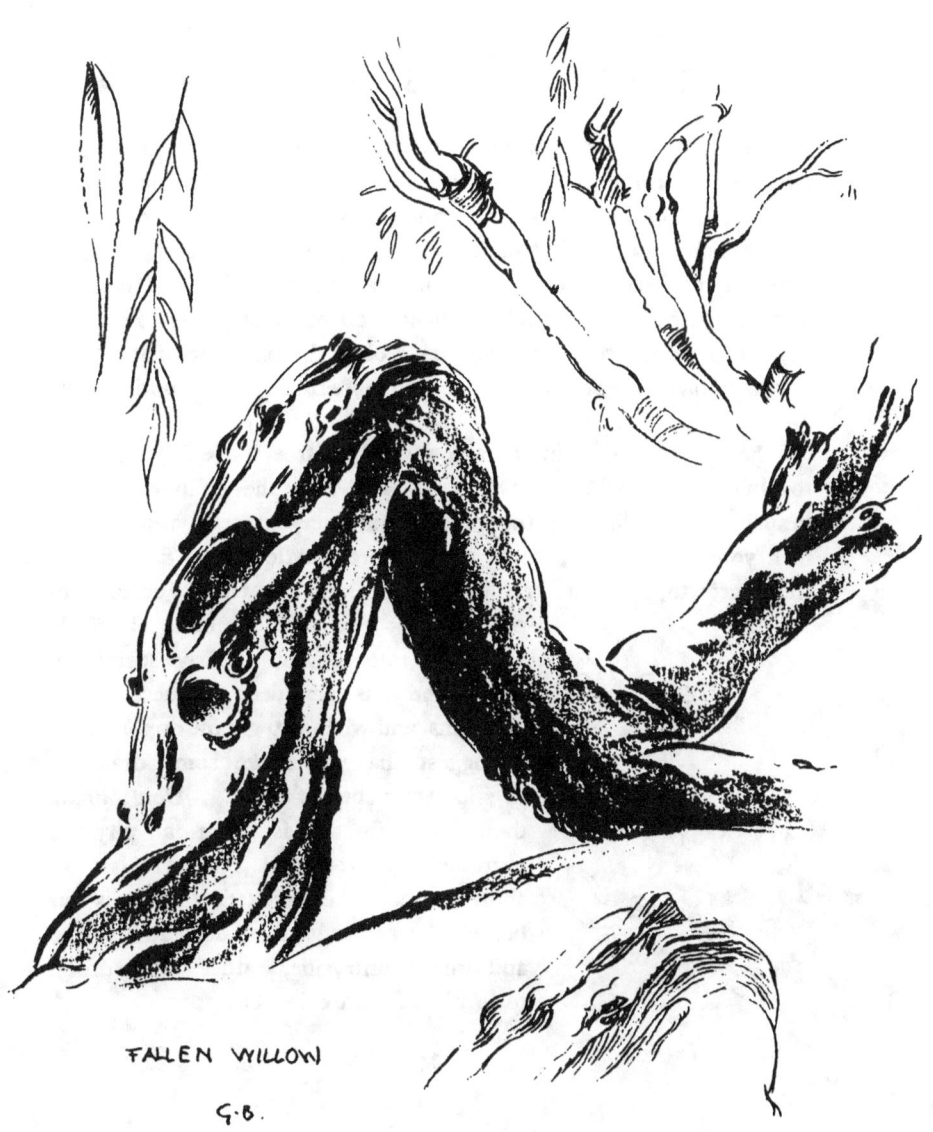

FALLEN WILLOW

G.B.

PLATE 10. LEAVES OF APPLE TREE

These are the leaves of the Wild Apple, which is the only Apple tree native to Britain. For drawing, the Apple leaf is particularly good. It is of a well-defined clean shape, and the twigs, from which it grows in little bunches, twist about in all sorts of interesting ways. There is no need for me to repeat the method of drawing them, for it is the same as that which I have already explained on previous pages. Probably you will have noticed, when you have been climbing one of the trees, that the leaves are smooth on top and sometimes downy underneath.

I have made a drawing of a young Apple tree (page 27) especially to show you how the leaves grow and how they join on to the branches. The lines of the branches are very graceful and sinuous in a young tree, but become much more erratic in the direction of their growth, as the tree becomes older. At the bottom of page 27 is a cluster of buds all ready to break into flower. Early spring in the country is heralded by these lovely blossoms, and when you get the opportunity, I suggest that you make some drawings of small branches of them. Don't break them off, for it is such a pity to mutilate any tree, and blossoms last so short a time when picked, that it is far better for us all to let them decorate the tree and the countryside, rather than droop forlornly in a vase in your room.

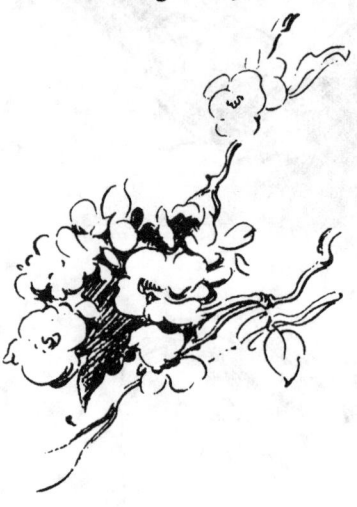

24

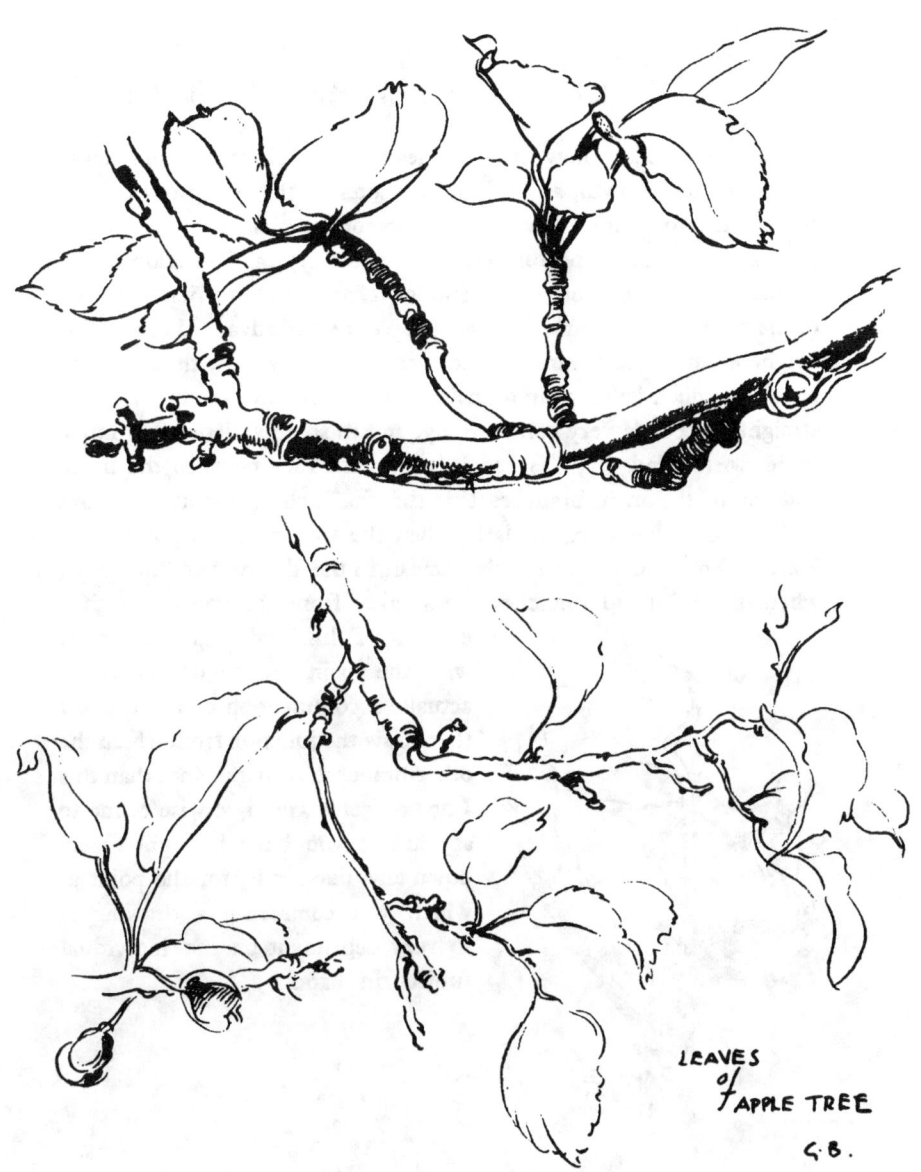

LEAVES
of
APPLE TREE

G.B.

PLATES 11 & 12. APPLE TREES

You can see below how the branches of the Apple tree become more erratic in their growth, as I said in the notes on the young tree. This tree is fairly old and I have drawn it before the leaves come, so that you may have the opportunity of seeing the typical formation of its characteristic branching. The sudden change in direction of many of the branches is a marked habit in apple trees of advanced age. The height of these trees varies from twenty to thirty feet, though some never get much larger than a bush. As you will see, the trunk is not straight but bends very considerably, and in some varieties it is much more twisted and very fissured. It is in the fork between the trunk and one of the main branches that the chaffinch and stonecock love to build their nests, particularly when the tree is growing near to a house. You will see the fork I mean in the drawing on this page, where the left-hand branches break away from the trunk. With a

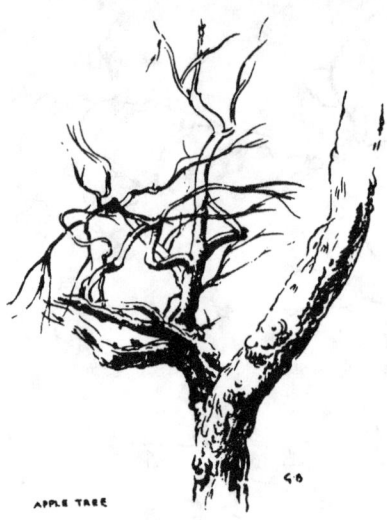

APPLE TREE

drawing of this kind, it is best to start with the main branch on the right, actually a continuation of the trunk ; then draw the junction from which the other branches spring. More than this I do not feel it would be wise of me to say and it would not be right to lay down any fixed rule, for the point at which you commence a drawing is so very dependant on the individual subject in hand.

26

YOUNG
APPLE TREE

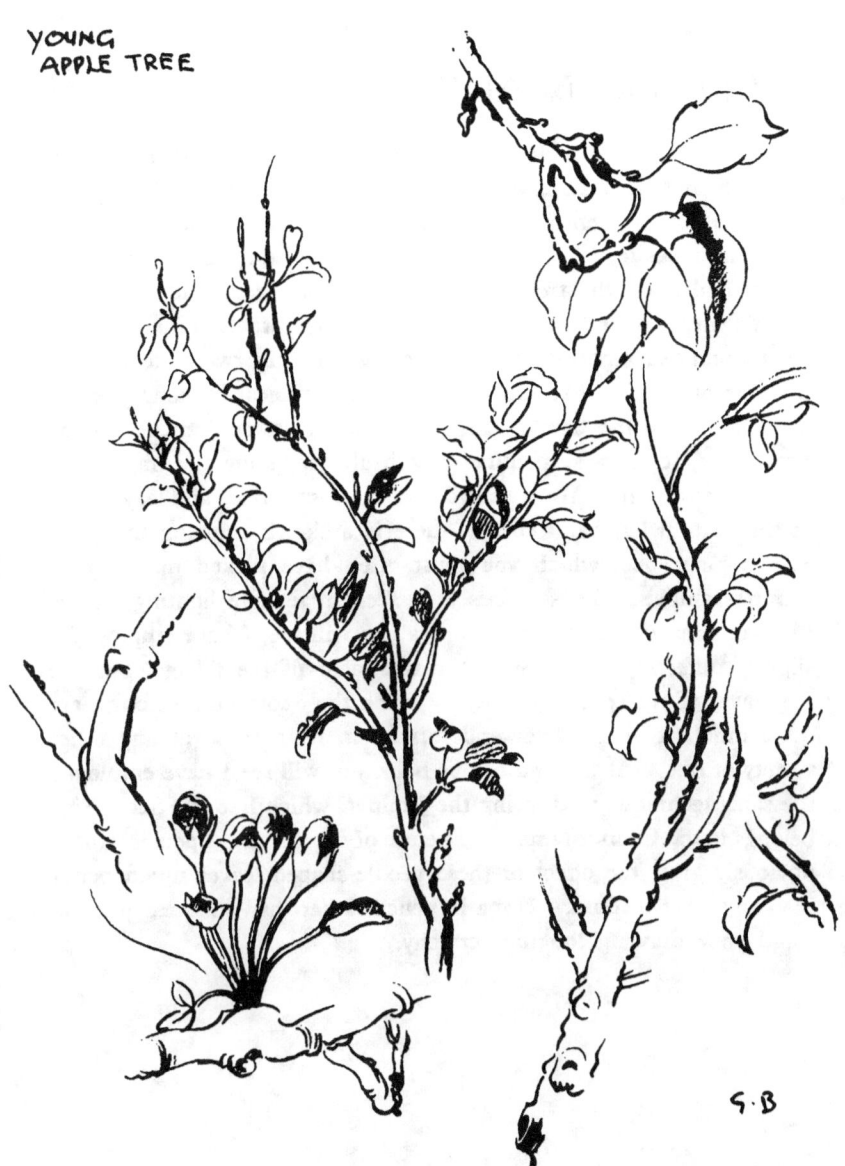

G·B

PLATE 13. BRANCH OF SCOTS PINE

Commonly, though incorrectly referred to as the Scotch Fir, this Pine tree is a very familiar sight crowning the crests of little hills, as well as in bracken-laden forests or woods. Its bark, a study of which is opposite, is of a rich copper colour and fairly smooth, as it gets higher up the tree, though towards the ground it is split up into patches, rather like crazy paving. In height, the Pine grows to about eighty or ninety feet, measuring as much as twelve feet round the bole or trunk. My illustration shows a typical branch, growing from low down the trunk. Like most of the lower branches of the Scots Pine, it has a serpentine growth almost giving the impression of rapid movement. Also I have drawn the winter buds and leaves, and in the bottom left-hand corner, there is a sketch showing the well-known pine cone, which you must often have picked up on your country rambles. These cones are excellent for fire lighting, as the Pine contains a quantity of resin. As you will see, I have employed a slightly different technique in the treatment of the foliage, because the leaves of the conifer family, to which the Scots Pine belongs, are quite different in character and formation, from those of any other variety of tree. At the end of this book you will see I have employed the same technique in drawing the Juniper, which like the Scots Pine belongs to the Conifer family. The use of short straight pencil strokes obviously gives the effect of these needle-shaped leaves much better than any other method. Use a B. pencil rather than a harder grade to avoid your drawing looking scratchy.

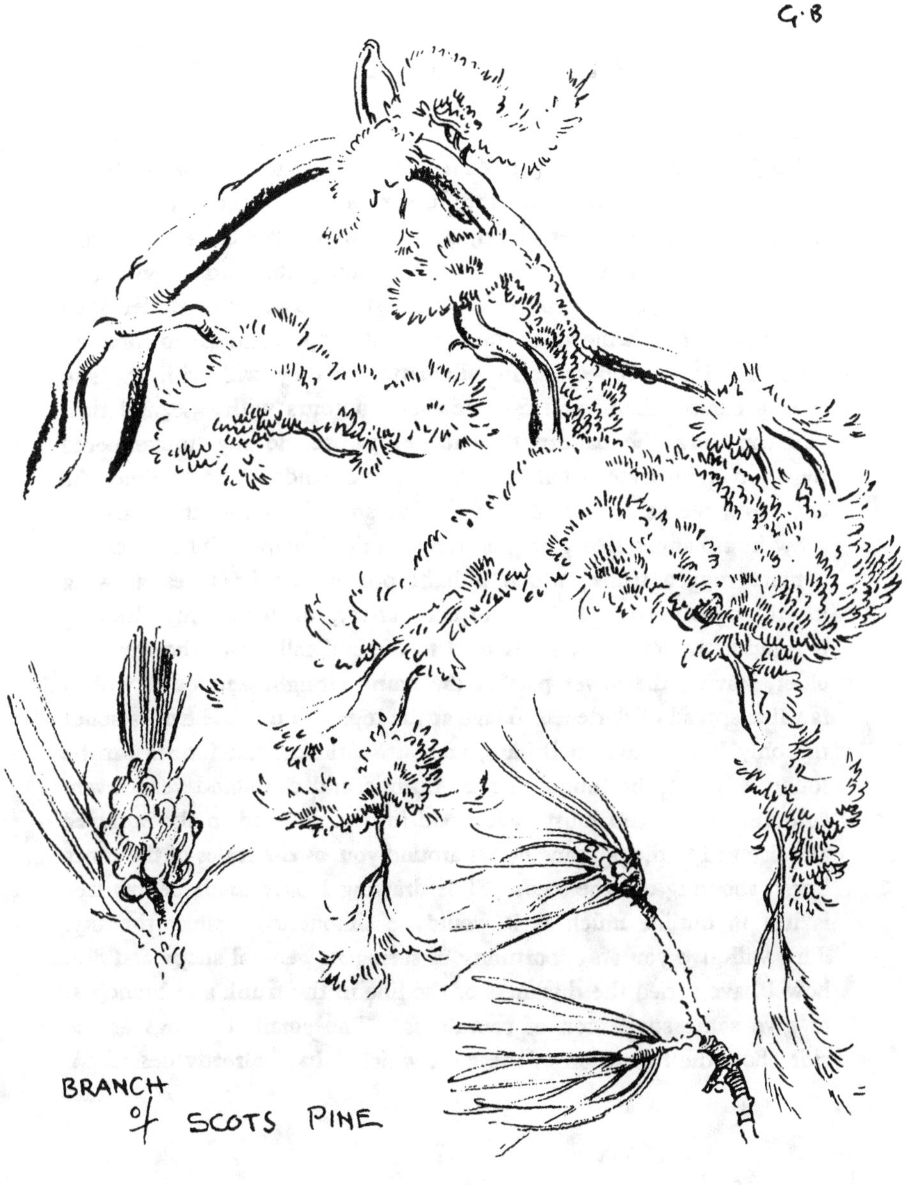

G.8

BRANCH of SCOTS PINE

PLATE 14. SCOTS PINE

As you will have noticed, the Scots Pine is a very tall tree attaining a height of some ninety feet. There is a very tall one, probably the tallest in England at Petworth, Sussex, and it reaches nearly one hundred and twenty feet in height. When you see these tall stately trees against an evening sunset, they look like grim sentinels guarding the country beyond. The effect is most imposing, and under such conditions they will give you excellent opportunities to practise your drawing. Appearing in silhouette, as they will with the sun setting behind them, you can see their contours with ease, and then you can draw the pattern they make against the sky, unhampered by a lot of intricate detail. There are two kinds of Scots Pine, the one has a reddish coloured trunk, fairly smooth, whilst the branches grow in a manner that gives the tree a conical shape. The other has a more rugged trunk, which is light brown, the branches growing mostly downwards. In the former variety, of which my drawing is typical, the lower branches tend to die and fall off as the tree gets older, leaving the lower part of the trunk straight and bare, with a fan-like spread of flattened foliage at the top. This fine tree is about the only Pine native to Britain, and in Scotland, vast forests can be found. It is to be found all over Europe, and can stand very severe cold and wet. You must have stood in a pine-wood in the summer and listened to the popping noises around you, as the scales of the cones burst, shooting out the seeds. The drawing I have made of this tree is just in outline much as it would be silhouetted against the sky. This will give you an opportunity of seeing its general shape and also how I have varied the thickness of the line in the trunk and branches, to give some suggestion of roundness. The small drawings at the side show the formation of the bark which I have already described.

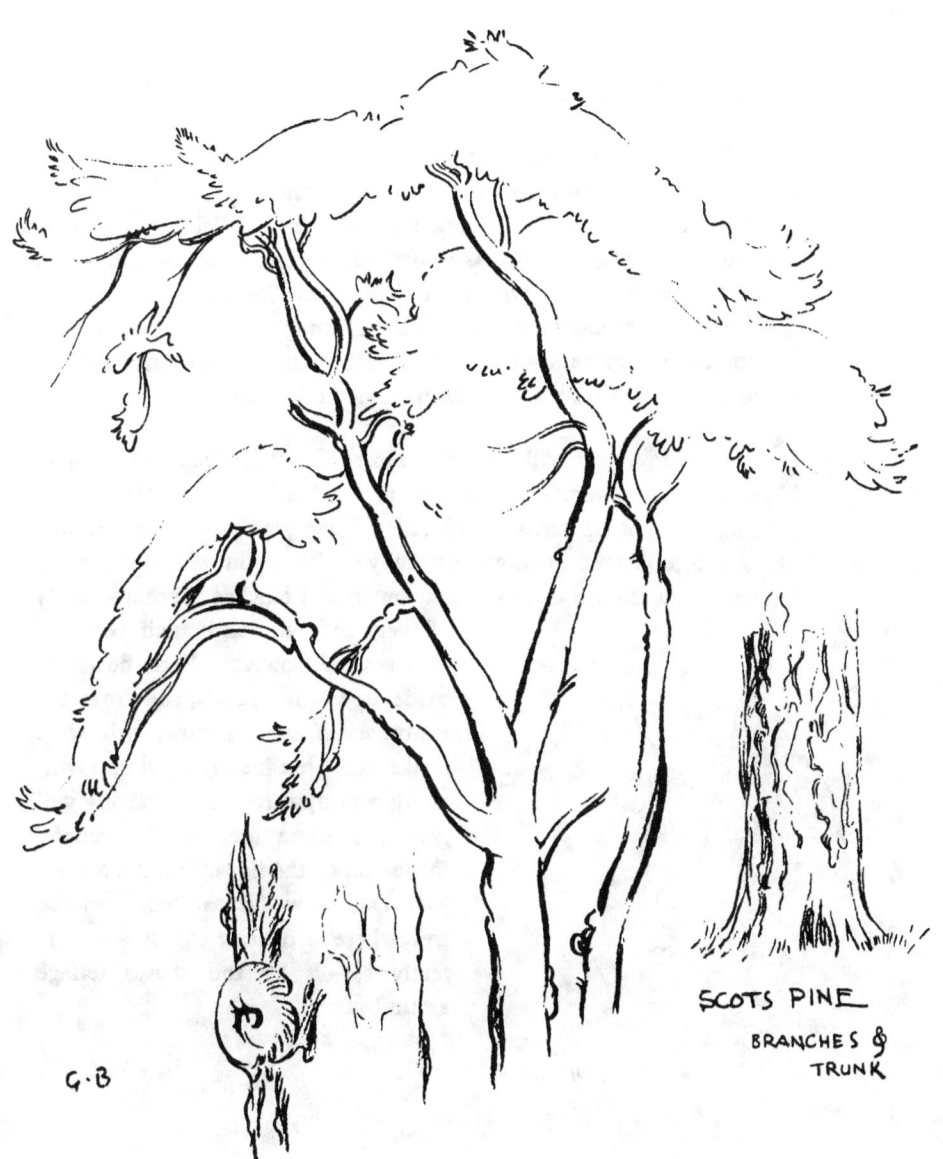

SCOTS PINE

BRANCHES &
TRUNK

G·B

PLATES 15 & 16.   CHESTNUT LEAF & BLOSSOM

Nothing could be more delightful to draw than Horse Chestnut leaves.   When growing on upright branches, they are at right-angles to the branch and on horizontal branches they lie parallel with them, so that you will always find their upper surface turned towards the sky. As these leaves are very large, the foliage of the Chestnut becomes very dense in summer and when arrayed in all the glory of its magnificent blossom, it is very handsome indeed.   When the leaves eventually fall, they leave a mark on the branch like a horseshoe.

During May, you will find the Horse Chestnut laden with lovely blossoms.   How very like candles on a Christmas tree they look, pointing straight upwards to the sky.   Have you ever examined one of these complicated blossoms carefully?   First you will see that the flowers grow from a central stalk, on little branches, perhaps thirty of them and on each branch you will find several flowers.   Each flower is made up of five petals, and from the centre seven stamens grow, with white stalks and pink heads, curving downwards and upwards.   My drawing will give you some idea of the general formation of the flower but it does not look half so well separated from the tree, where its delicate colour is so perfectly set-off by the dense foliage around it.

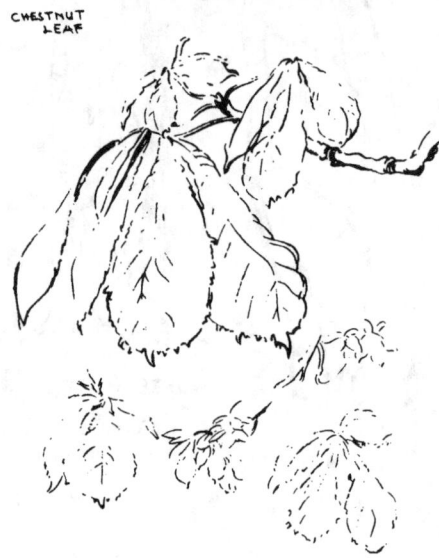

CHESTNUT
LEAF

32

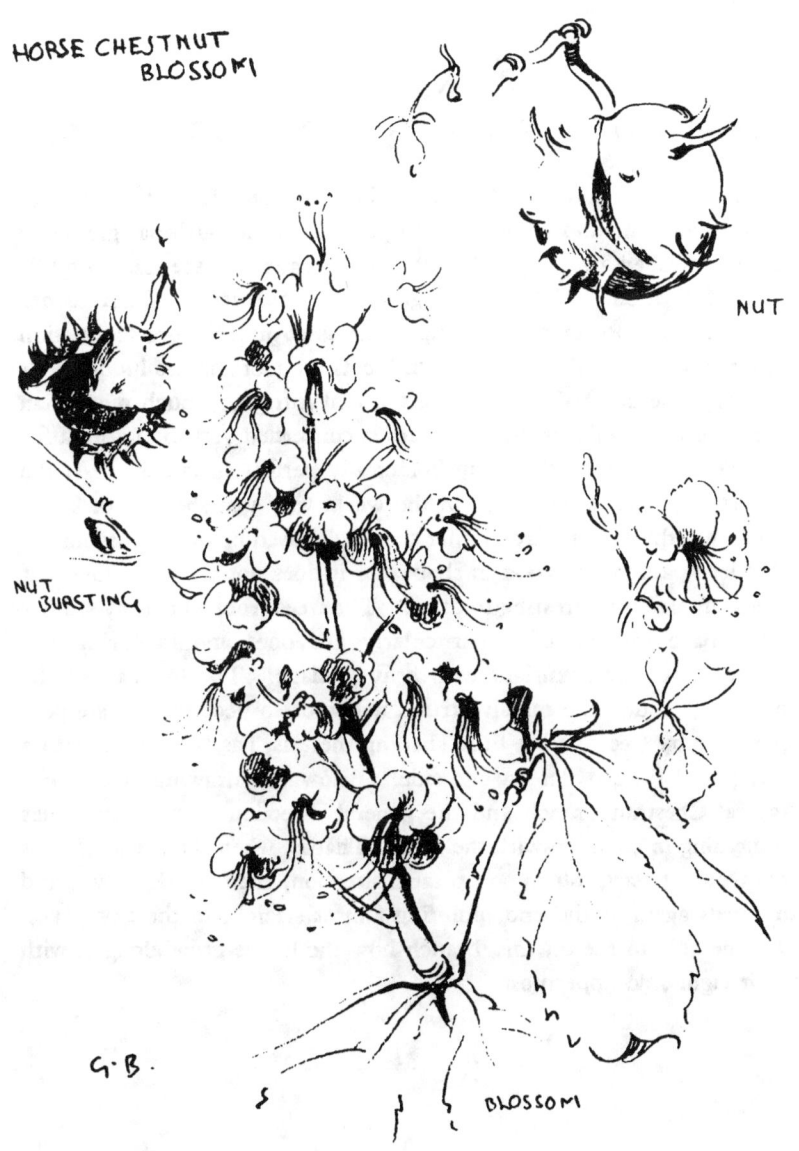

HORSE CHESTNUT
BLOSSOM

NUT

NUT
BURSTING

G·B·

BLOSSOM

PLATE 17.

CHESTNUT — TRUNK, ROOTS AND BRANCH

There are a number of Horse Chestnuts on Hampstead Heath, growing on a mound beside a small pond. As the earth has gradually become washed away from the roots, it is possible to see their complicated formation. When the beginning of the roots of a tree are exposed, as those in my drawing, there is so much more fascination in drawing the trunk, than when the roots are more or less hidden. It is always the unusual and unexpected that intrigues, much more than the normal. So far as drawing trees is concerned you should look for interesting shapes, rather than botanically perfect specimens. At the same time, there is no reason in the world why you should not select a fine healthy-looking tree rather than a diseased or dying one but see that it is particularly good in shape, for it does not always follow that a healthy tree is interesting to draw. The trees from which my studies were made happen to be particularly fine ones, and in spring and summer they are luxuriant with heavy foliage. The top half of the next page shows the massive trunk and root so necessary to support this weighty tree. What little shading there is, has been done with a soft pencil rubbed flat on one side. Below this drawing is one of a typical Chestnut branch and the general direction of its growth has something in common with the Ash. That is, when the branch leaves the trunk it starts off in an upward direction, then bends down, and upwards again at the end, pointing almost straight to the sky. You will be able to see on this branch how the leaves grow along it with their right side uppermost.

34

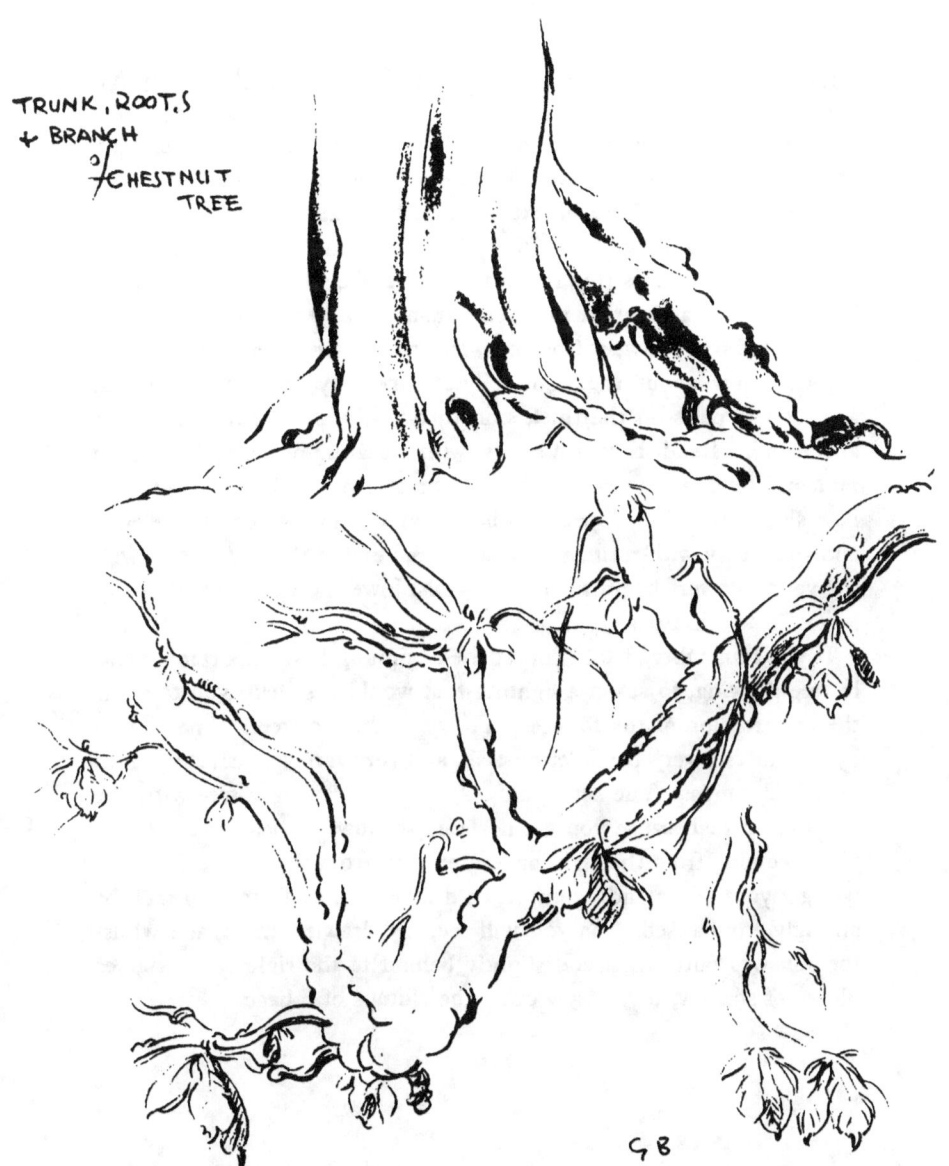

TRUNK, ROOTS
& BRANCH
of CHESTNUT
TREE

G B

PLATE 18. CHESTNUT TREE IN FULL LEAF

I seem to have told you so much about the Horse Chestnut already that there seems little left to tell. Leaves, blossoms, roots and trunk have all had their share of explanation, but there still remain some interesting facts about the buds. Before starting on this, you might like to know that this tree reaches a height of eighty feet and that the bark is smooth and rather more grey than green in colour. It is in no way related to the Sweet Chestnut, the fruit of which, as you know, is edible. Now about the buds. These are very large and pointed, arranged in pairs on the thick smooth twigs, with an extra large one at the end. Reddish brown scales, with a coating of resin, cover each bud, and towards the end of March the sun melts the resin and the new shoots begin to appear. The shoots are pinky red at the ends and still sticky with resin. From the large bud at the end of the twig, the young flowers begin to appear, whilst lower down the fresh young leaves grow in pairs.

If you remember, I told you at the beginning how important it was in tree drawing, to select a lighting that would best help you to show the construction of the foliage. To try to draw a tree in line, not lit by the sun is a very bewildering task, and very rarely satisfactory even in skilled hands. The same thing applies to drawing a tree with the sun full on it, because you get no large shadows to help you. If the sun is coming from the right or left, or even from slightly behind, you will get your tree standing out in bold relief and its formation will be strongly emphasised. As you will see, my drawing was made whilst the sun was fairly high and slightly behind to the right. This gives plenty of shadow, to " throw out " the clumps of foliage.

36

HORSE CHESTNUT
in FULL LEAF

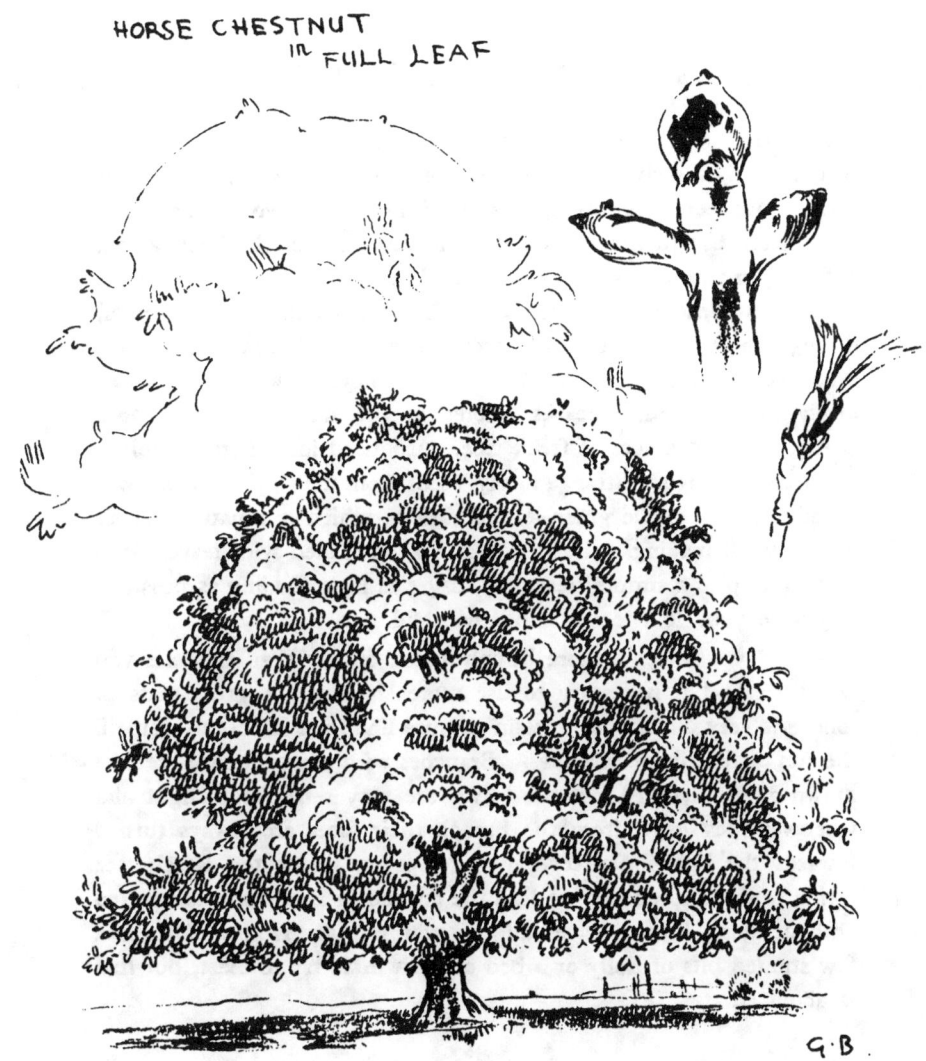

G·B·

PLATE 19. LEAVES OF BEECH TREE

The mention of Beech leaves usually conjures up a picture of golden autumn, and calls vividly to mind the pleasant rustling sound which is made as our feet wade through masses of them in the woods in autumn or winter. But in the spring, these leaves are a bright fresh green, changing in summer to a much darker hue, and in common with the Oak, a few dead ones withered and brown, remain on the tree all through the winter. The lower branches, when laden with leaves, droop nearly to the ground, like the ones I have drawn here. Those lovely copper-coloured leaves belong, as you know, to the Copper Beech, which is a sort of freak tree, introduced into England only a hundred years ago. Strange to say, seeds from the Copper Beech will usually grow into the green-leaved variety, which is a native British tree. When making a drawing of a branch loaded with leaves, it is best to keep to a simple treatment, using as little shading as possible, otherwise your foliage will look too solid.

Should you select a more heavily laden branch than this one you will then find it necessary to use more shading. A great mass of foliage is very difficult to explain in pure line so it is best to wait till the sun casts suitable shadows. Branches with scanty foliage are best drawn as in Plate 19. Beech leaves are very sensitive to light and wherever they grow from the branch their faces are always turned towards the light. Scarcely anything grows under the Beech tree owing to the drip and so we find the ground in Beech woods covered with decaying brown leaves all the year round. Here and there a few stunted bits of holly or a bed of Periwinkle try to exist, but that is about all.

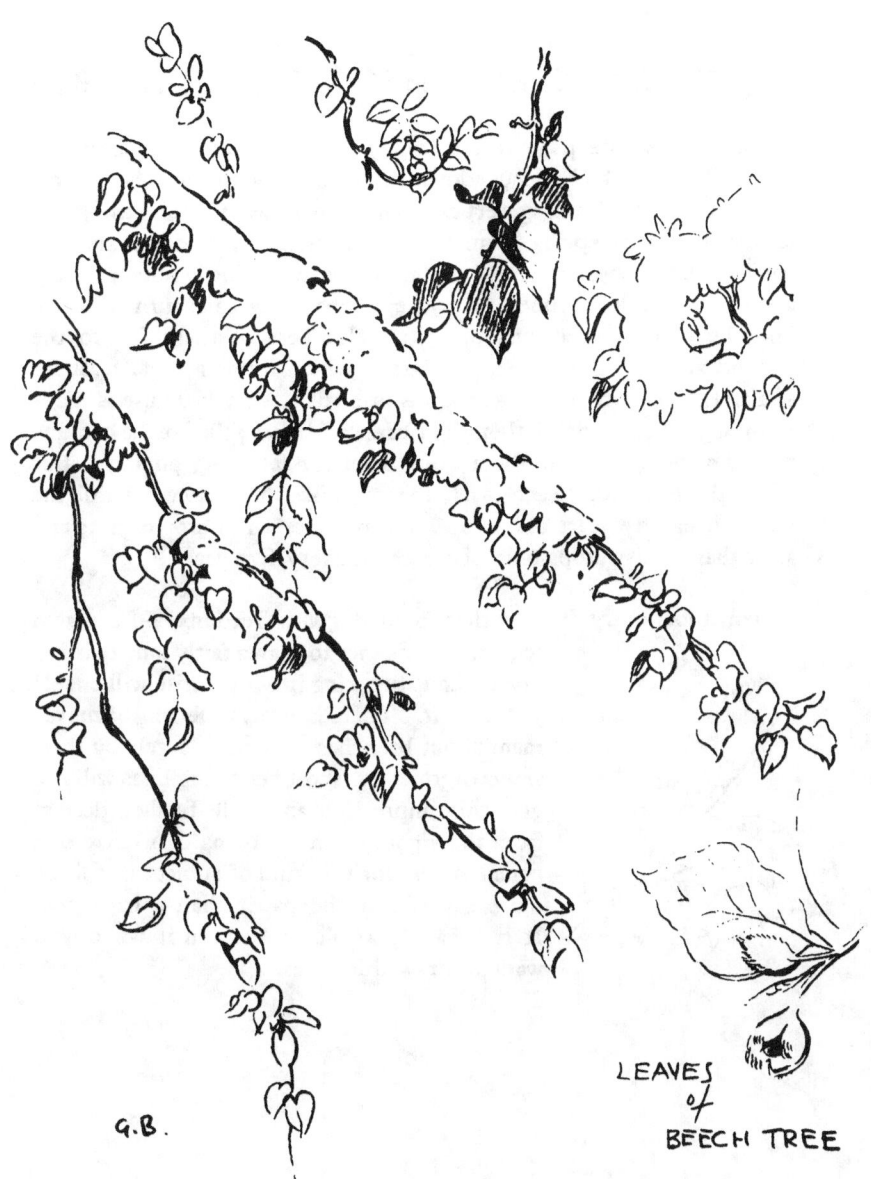

G.B.

LEAVES
of
BEECH TREE

PLATE 20. BRANCHES OF BEECH TREE

On the opposite page is a drawing of one of the lower branches of the Beech, which bends downwards towards the ground. How very much like writhing serpents, and how heavy and strong the shoots look that spring from the main branch. Hidden amongst the foliage on these branches, we find thousands of little nuts, growing about the middle of June, and by September they have turned brown and the outer coat begins to split. Numbers of them fall to the ground and are called " Beech-Mast ", which forms a royal feast for squirrels, doormice, and many kinds of birds. Very little use is made of these nuts in England, though in France I believe they make cooking oil from them, and use them quite a lot for fattening poultry. But of all the lovers of Beech-mast, the pig takes first place. Until the tree is over fifty years old, it does not produce a full crop of nuts and after that similar crops only occur about every five years.

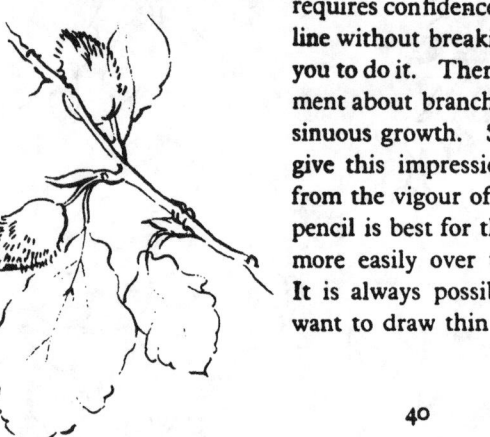

Remember to try drawing these branches with freedom. Of course it requires confidence to draw a fairly long twisting line without breaking it but practise will enable you to do it. There is always a feeling of movement about branches suggested largely by their sinuous growth. Short hesitating lines will not give this impression and will further detract from the vigour of the drawing. A fairly soft pencil is best for this kind of subject as it flows more easily over the paper than a hard one. It is always possible to sharpen it when you want to draw thin lines.

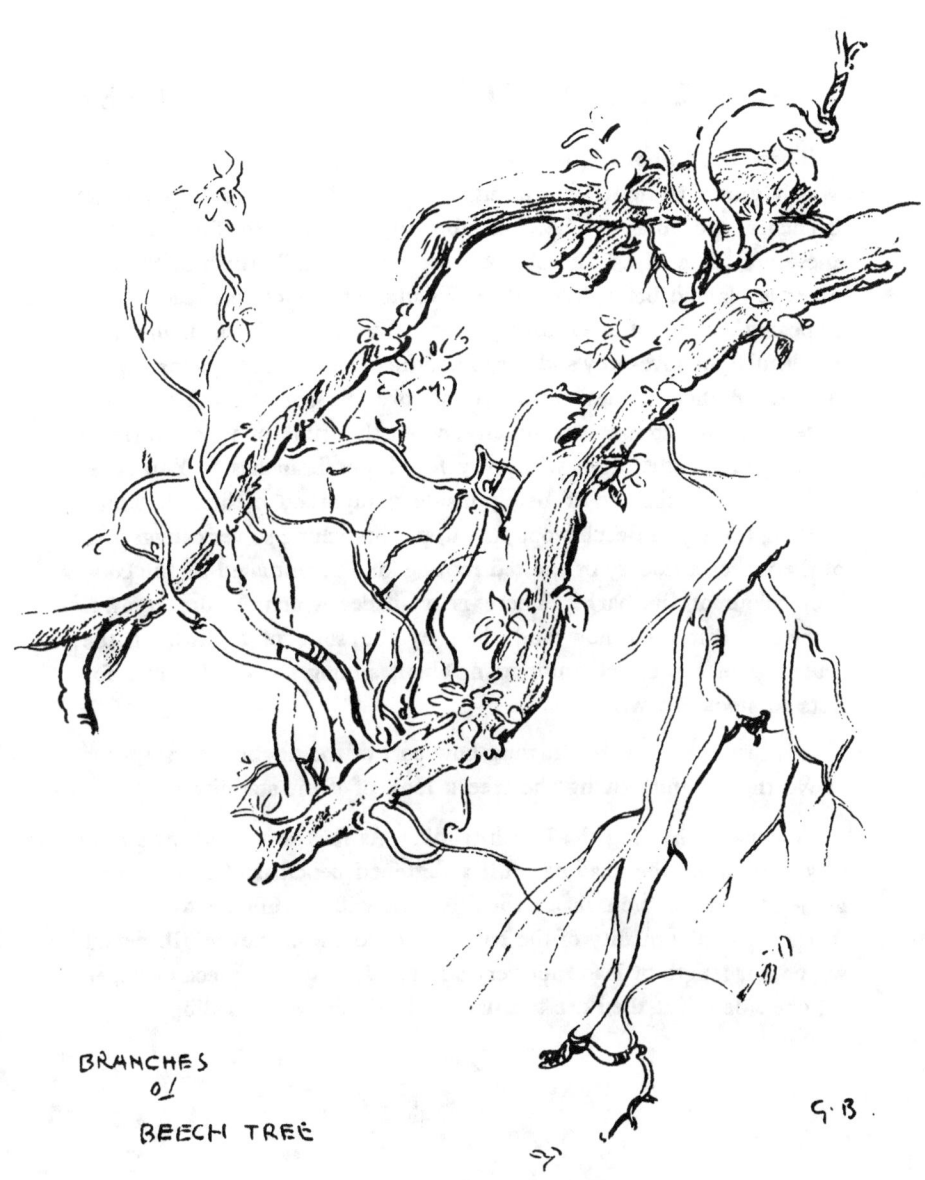

BRANCHES
o/
BEECH TREE

G·B·

PLATE 21. TRUNK OF BEECH TREE

There is a famous Queen Beech in Ashridge Park, Hertfordshire, which grows straight up for eighty feet and then spreads out its branches and foliage. Beeches abound at Burnham Beeches, and these are some of the finest specimens, while in Perthshire there is a hedge planted before the battle of Culloden, which has reached the imposing height of over ninety feet. The bark of the trunk is a beautiful light dove-grey and very smooth, so irresistible to young lovers, who carve their names or initials all over its surface. There is a stately, almost monumental quality, about the trunk of a Beech, rising to its great height often with very few lower branches. You must have had that feeling of being inside a dignified cathedral, whilst walking through a Beech wood, the upper branching so very suggestive of the intricate tracery of vaulted roofing, and accentuated by the cool, grey colour of the bark. There is a silence which is almost awe-inspiring, disturbed now and then by the song of a bird, or the scufflings of a squirrel, rummaging about among the dead leaves for nuts to stock his winter larder.

It is easy to see in the drawing how part of the mighty roots appear above the ground, giving the tree a look of great stability.

Now about drawing the Beech trunk. As it is so smooth, the best way is to apply the shading with a flattened pencil, and a fairly soft grade at that. If you shade with lines, it will be difficult to present that almost silky quality of the bark. Take a 2B. or even 3B. pencil with a fair length of lead, not very sharp. Rub it on a piece of paper till one side is flat then use the flattened side for your shading.

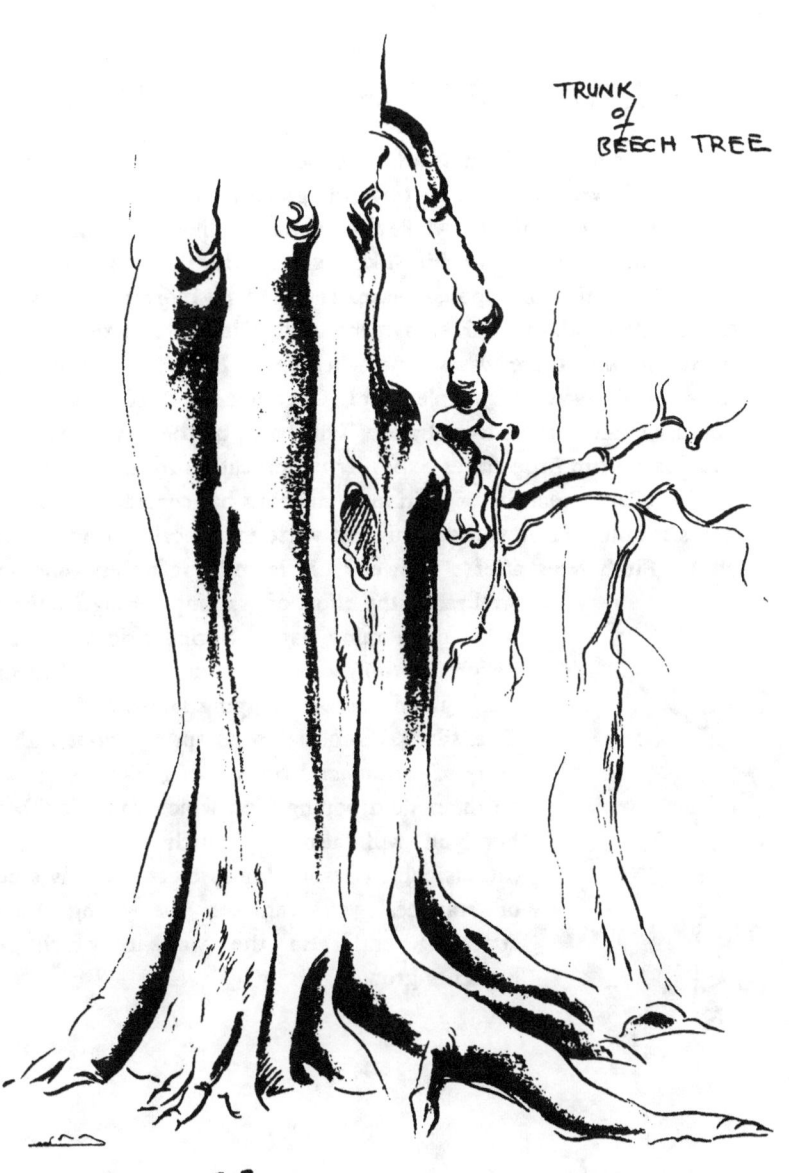

TRUNK
of
BEECH TREE

G·B·

PLATE 22.   BRANCHES OF SILVER BIRCH

For a vision of daintiness and elegance, there is no tree to compare with the Silver Birch.   The tiny soft green leaves quiver and dance in the light, making the whole tree shimmer like a fountain in the sun.   In spite of all this fairy-like delicacy, the Birch is quite hardy and will flourish in exposed places shunned by more robust-looking trees.   Don't allow your enjoyment of this lovely tree to be spoilt, by recollecting there was a time when the " Birch " had a meaning for you which was far from pleasant ! Of course the chief characteristic, familiar to all, is the silvery bark.   This bark, by the way, is very thin and peals off in little flakes exposing underneath a fresh silvery layer. Having a large quantity of resin in it, the bark has considerable powers to resist rain.   Have you ever noticed what an agreeable scent is given off by Birch trees after a shower ?   It is most refreshing and will well repay the effort of walking through a Birch-wood on a rainy day.   Spring brings so many delightful things to the countryside, blossoms, fresh green leaves, skipping lambs and catkins. The. silver Birch makes its spring debut with an array of catkins and fresh young leaves.   It will be the male drooping kind which you know best, but you will also see much smaller female catkins, which stand almost erect.   In my study of branches you can see the young leaves appearing and also the way in which the branches grow.

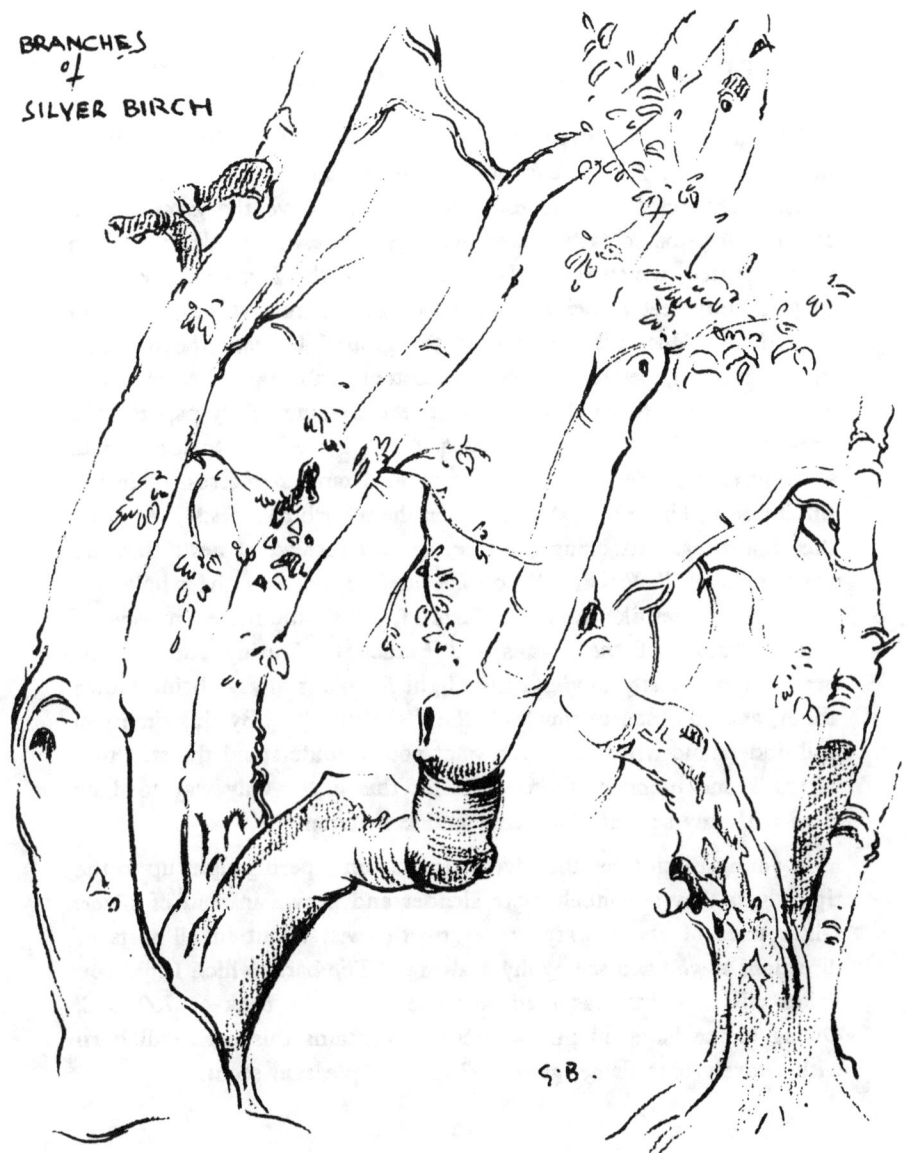

BRANCHES
of
SILVER BIRCH

S·B·

PLATE 23. TRUNKS OF SILVER BIRCH

This drawing will give you an opportunity of seeing how the Birch grows from the ground and how the bark has those dark markings, called "lenticels". The roots spread out above the ground in a sort of splay-footed fashion and are very interesting to draw. When fully matured, which takes about fifty years, the Birch will be about fifty to sixty feet in height, and before the century is passed it will have died. Moss often grows on the ground beneath the tree, and in the autumn, peculiar crimson toadstools will appear, from which a substance is extracted and used in the making of fly-papers. As these toadstools are very poisonous it will be as well to leave them severely alone. Perhaps you have noticed tangled masses up in the Birch tree and have probably mistaken them for bird's nests. Actually this is a disease attacking the tree, so that instead of nests they are what is called "Witches'-Brooms." Before drawing the whole tree or groups of trees like the one on Plate 24, you should make a number of careful studies of the trunks and branches. During summer the branches are mostly hidden as the light foliage is always being blown about, and so obscures much of the "skeleton." By this time you will understand why I so much want you to understand the structure of trunk and branches thoroughly, for this is the only way to draw trees with any sort of confidence and conviction.

In young Birch trees the silvery trunks run tapering right up to the tip, whilst they are much more slender and brown instead of silver. Older trees of about sixty years growth twist about in all sorts of directions as you will see by my drawing. The bark, which I told you flakes off in strips was used to write on as far back as 700 B.C. Owing to the large quantity of resin it contains this bark will burn with a lovely blue flame, giving off its very pleasant scent.

46

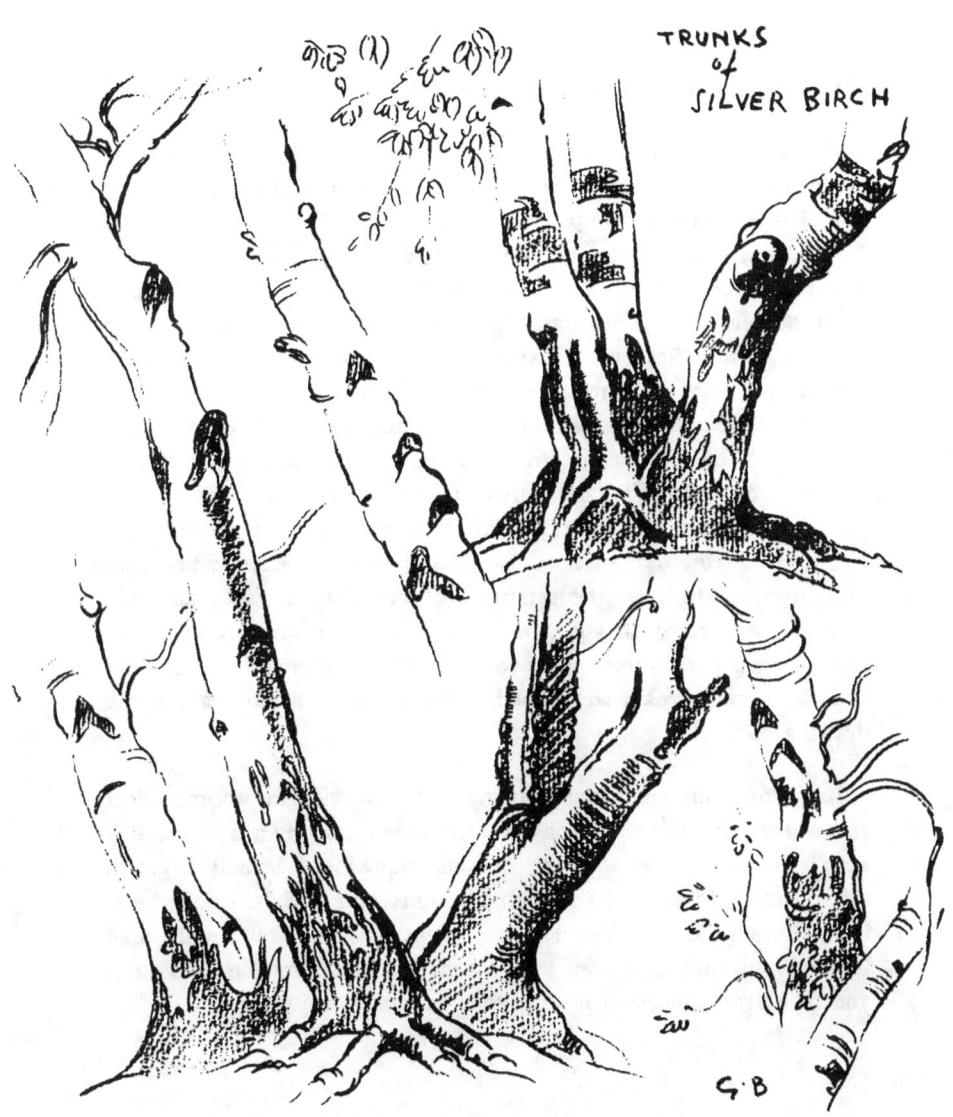

TRUNKS
of
SILVER BIRCH

PLATE 24. BIRCH TREE IN FULL LEAF

There is little more to say about the Birch and its habits, so I can devote this page to telling you more about the method of drawing it. Here we have a group of Silver Birch in full leaf. You see, as I told you, most of the branches are hidden completely and only the trunks remain visible. The delicate foliage hangs like plumage from the slender branches and twigs, and as the leaves are not large and dense, like the Elm and Chestnut, it is not so easy to obtain very definite contrasts of light and shade. However, if you get them in a favourable light and draw them from a fair distance, you will, by careful observation, be able to discern " groups " of leaves, forming masses which catch the light and throw relative shadows. The slender shoots which project from the main body of foliage, prevent the tree from looking like a heavy shapeless mass, and the lower branches drooping gracefully to the ground are very characteristic, and will help you very much in your drawings. The line round the outside of the trees is not continuous, as you will see. At intervals it is broken, and the pencil strokes are varied in thickness to avoid making the drawing look flat.

In making this particular drawing I started with the topmost leaf and worked downwards to the trunks. When drawing a tree which is mainly foliage, that is with few branches showing, I usually begin in this manner. Should you find that it suits you to begin elsewhere, by all means do so. There is one point however you should take into account, that is, as you start a somewhat full drawing at the top you then avoid smearing it with your hand as you proceed.

48

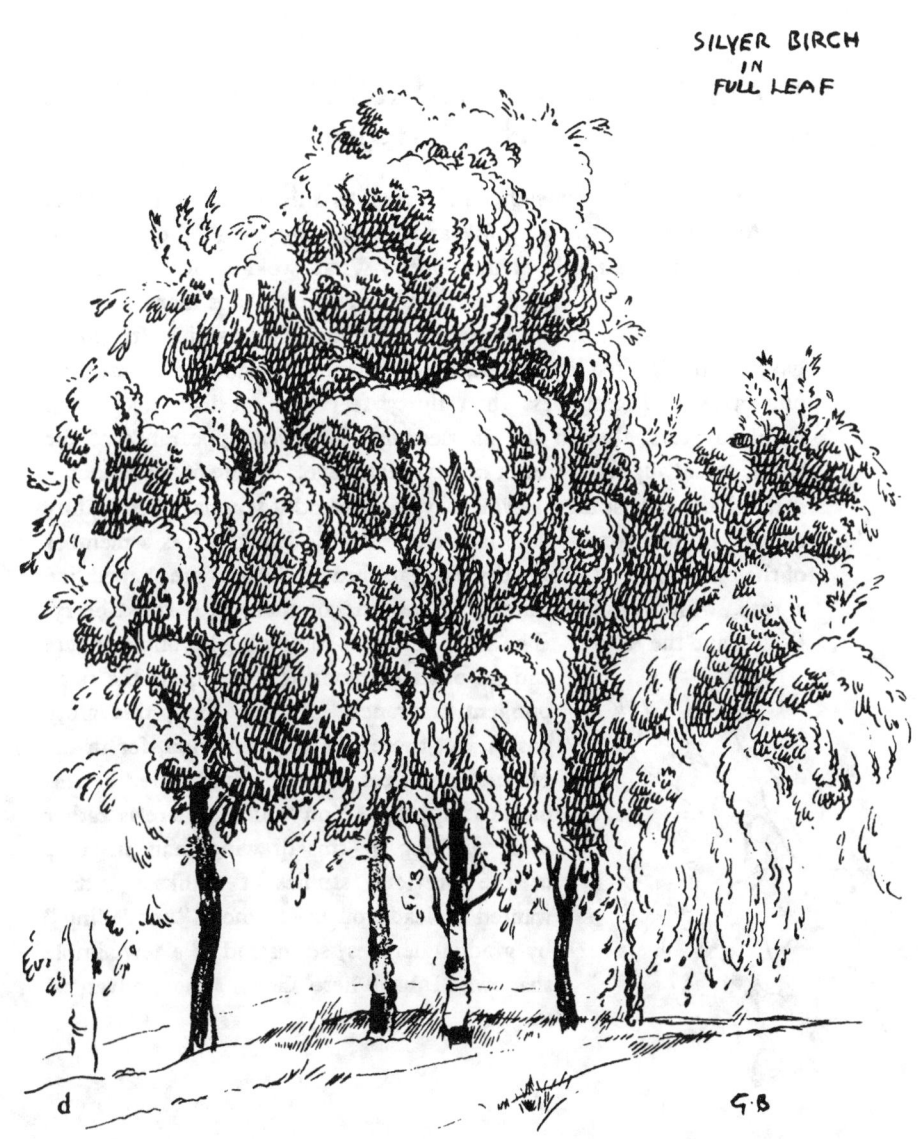

SILVER BIRCH
IN
FULL LEAF

d

G·B

PLATE 25. TRUNK AND ROOTS OF MAY TREE (HAWTHORN)

One of the loveliest sights in spring, is the abundant blossom of the May tree, spreading a pink and white mantle over the fields and hedges of the English countryside. What we are accustomed to call a May tree is, of course, a Hawthorn, and perhaps more than any other tree, it is bound up with the traditions of England. Its glories have been recorded by Chaucer, Milton and Swinburne to mention only a few. Mostly less than thirty feet high, it lives about two hundred years, though the gnarled and furrowed appearance of the trunk would suggest a tree of much greater age. Some of the branches carry sharp little spines, as you may have found if you have been guilty enough to pick some of the blossom. As the Hawthorn is a member of the rose family, it is not surprising to find the flowers are shaped like a rose, which circumstance it shares in common with the Cherry, Rowan and the Apple. The scent of May is something beyond compare

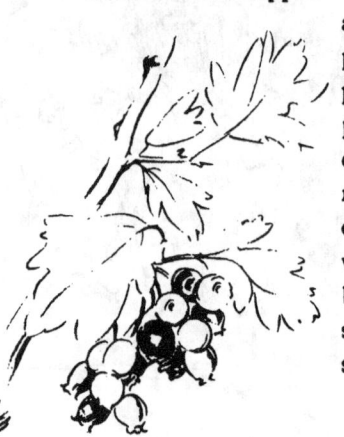

and no other common tree has quite the same pungent fragrance. All too soon, this glory passes, yet there is a compensation, for in the place of countless flowers, countless red berries or Haws appear. You will see there is rather more shading in this drawing than in some of the previous studies of trunks. I have wanted to lead you up to more " modelling " by gradual degrees, so instead of a few simple shadows, I have here shown a more advanced stage.

50

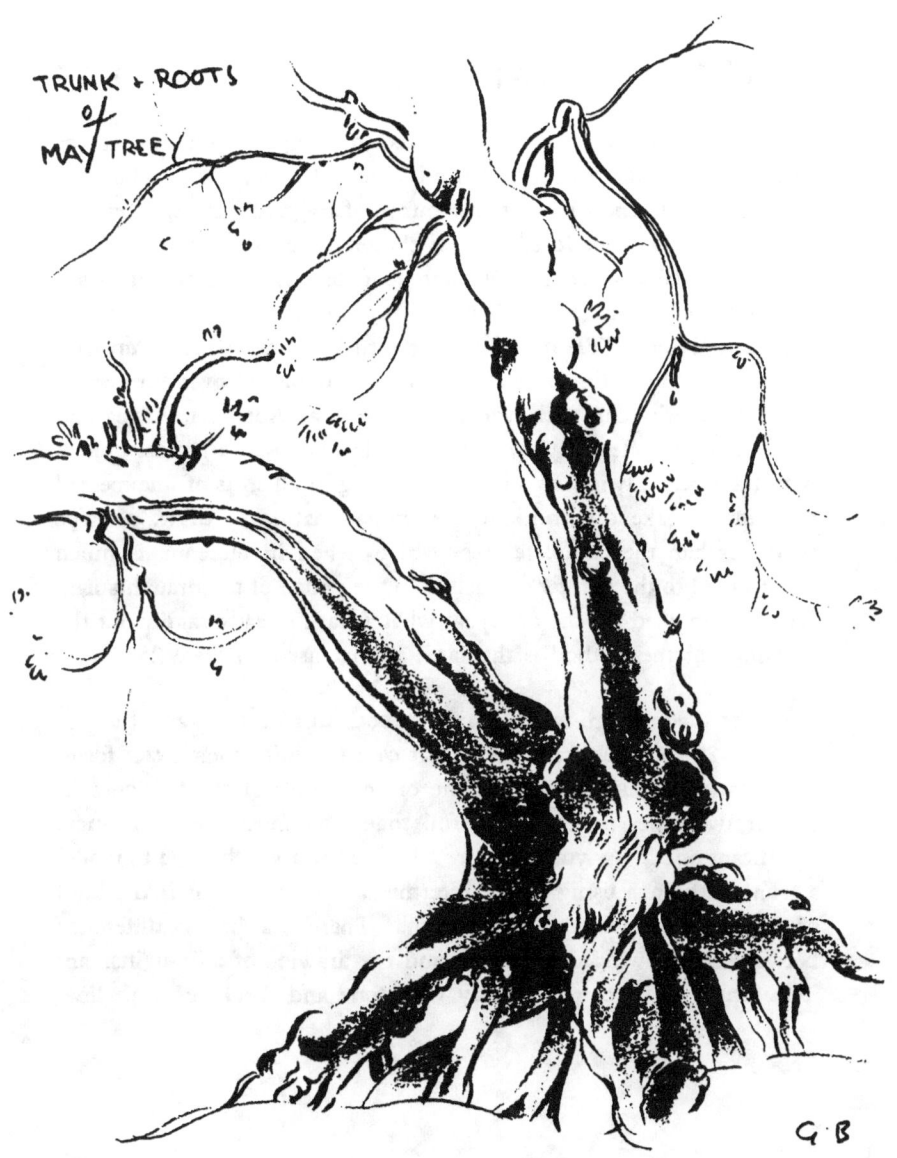

TRUNK + ROOTS
of
MAY TREE

G·B

PLATE 26. BRANCHES OF MAY TREE

Many years ago the first of May used to be a general holiday in the country, when the villagers danced round the May-pole. The top of the pole was ornamented with a bunch of fragrant May blossom and so was the head of the fortunate lass chosen to be May Queen. Those were great days, when the fun and laughter ran high and it was a matter of some moment whether the May would bloom in time for the annual festivities. Though the Hawthorn is so much bound up with the country life of England, it is also to be found all over Europe, as far north as Sweden and even as far afield as Australia, Africa and Western Asia. Here, in my drawing, I have chosen a typical branch with interlocked twigs, twisting and turning in all sorts of unexpected directions. Like the trunk, it is very fascinating to draw, perhaps more so than the complete tree, which, when in blossom, is much more suited to the painter's brush than the pencil of the draughtsman. There is no need for me to repeat what I have already said about the drawing, for the method is the same as that used on Plate 25.

As the shadows are fairly simple in both this drawing and the one on Plate 25 you must take very great care to notice their exact form. If you wish to suggest the volume or roundness of the branches in one or two tones instead of in full tone, you must select the most significant ones. As you get more advanced you will be able to model a trunk or branch using all the intermediary tones. This is the kind of drawing mostly used to paint from. There is a distinct difference between the drawing of a painter and the drawing of a draughtsman. The former is concerned mainly with tone and the latter with line.

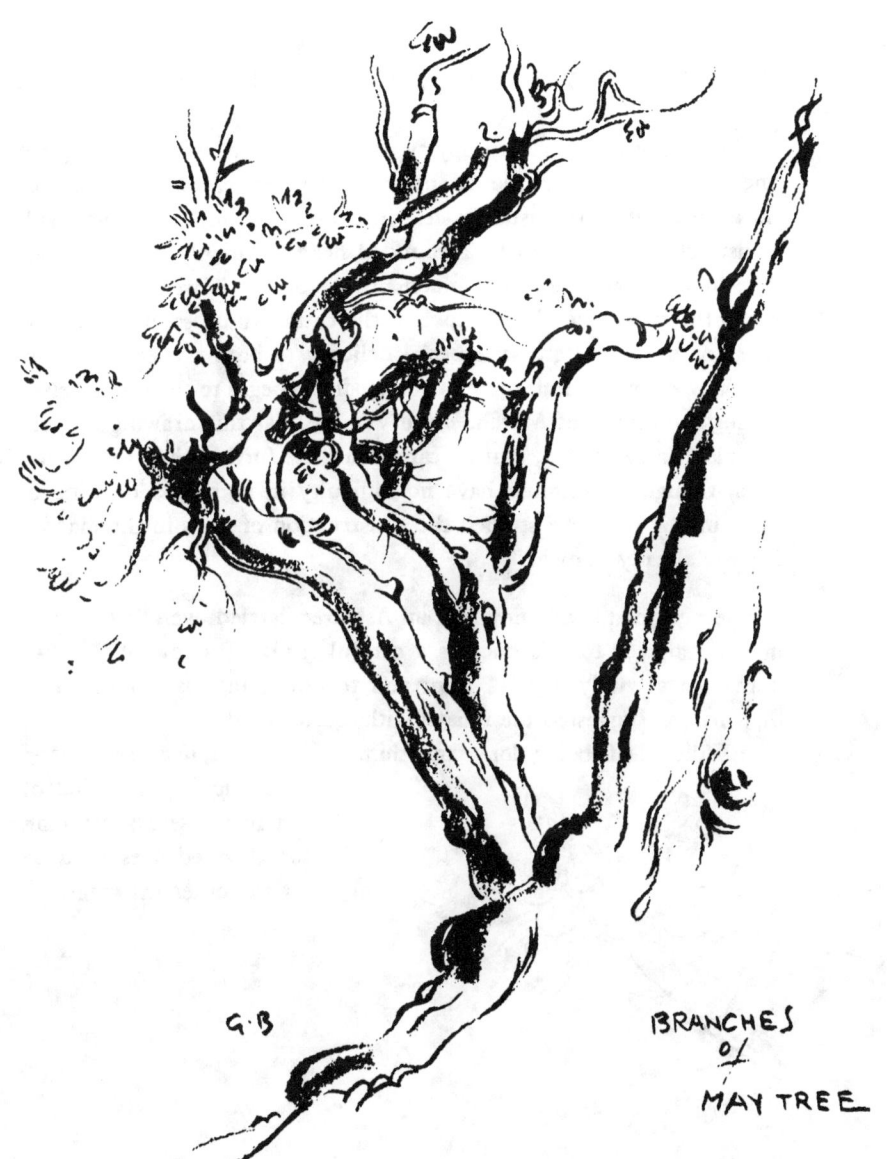

G·B   BRANCHES
of
MAY TREE

PLATE 27. MAY TREE IN LEAF

This is not the usual stumpy type of tree found in the hedges, but one that has escaped the attention of the hedger's shears. Under these fortunate circumstances it will grow to about forty feet, with a distinct trunk, topped by a rounded head of thickly tangled twigs. The lobed leaves vary very much in size, and if it were not for the sharp thorns on the older branches, the cattle would soon devour the tree, for the leaves are an especial delicacy to both horses and cows. Breaking early into leaf, the first young shoots begin to show themselves during the month of March. You will see that this drawing is more complete in execution, that is, carried a little further than the former ones, though you should have no difficulty in making a drawing of this kind, if you have studied the construction of trees in the manner I have already shown.

The next plate will show you an Ash tree carried even further, and in the endpiece to this book is a careful study of a row of Willows drawn on a windy day. I want you to notice in this last drawing, that I have suggested the foliage with quite a different sort of line. The Willow leaf being long and thin, as you will have seen, long thin lines suggest this kind of leaf seen in masses, better than the short hooked ones used in many of the other drawings.

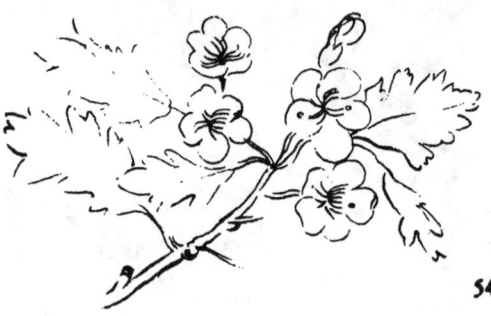

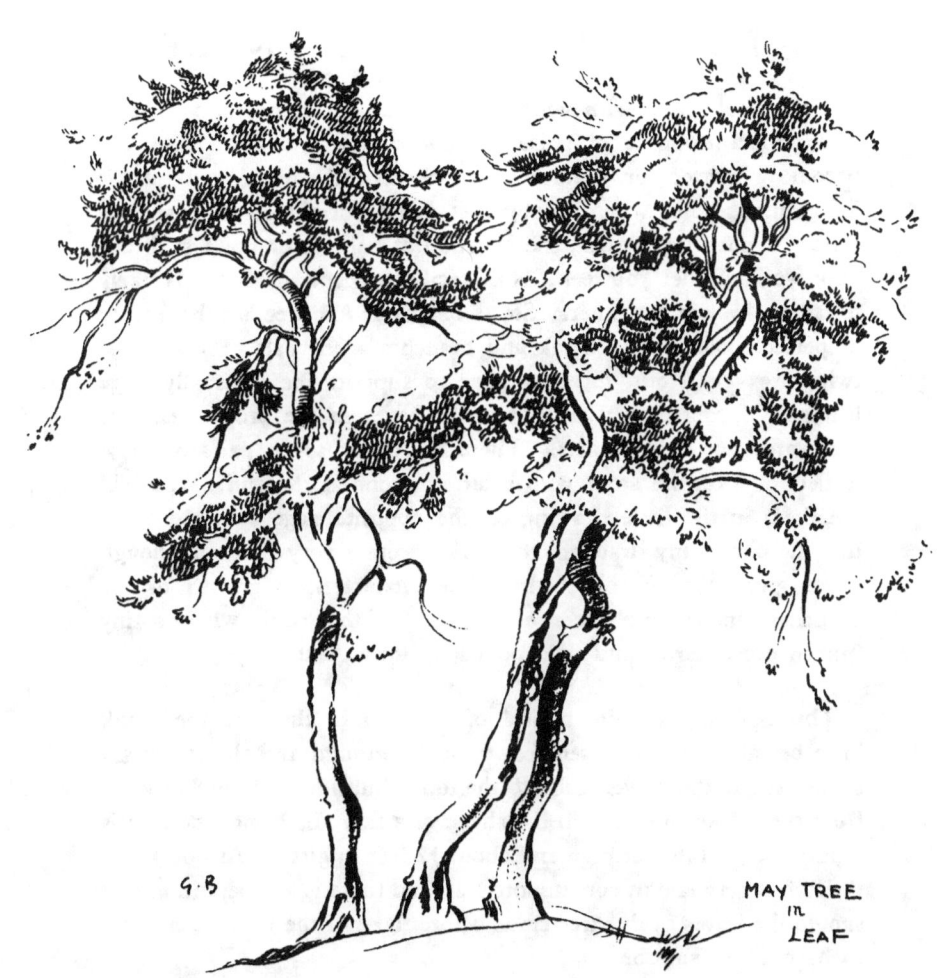

G·B

MAY TREE
in
LEAF

PLATE 28. ASH TREE IN LEAF

This stately tree, with what I should call an aristocratic bearing, is a perfect example of poise without symmetry. Poise does not become a matter for wonder in a symmetrical object, you take it for granted. But when an object standing upright on its base, like a tree, is not symmetrical, the question of balance or poise is forced upon you. Either you feel it is perfectly balanced, or that it is likely to fall one way or the other. So, as I say, our Ash tree has the quality of perfect poise. The trunk and branches are a pale grey and the twigs are very stout, for they have to support the unusually large leaves. Of course they are not really leaves in the proper sense of the word, but only leaflets. There are about seven pairs of these leaflets on a central stem, with a terminal one at the end. You will see them in the little drawing on the opposite page. In old trees, like the one in my drawing, the bark becomes very fissured, though never gnarled as in old Oaks. The characteristic growth of the branches can be clearly seen on the right of the trunk, where a tiny branch grows down and then points up towards the sky.

This drawing is quite typical of the Ash in the way the trunk branches about eight or ten feet from the ground and the two main stems ascend almost vertically to the top. Subsiduary branches grow from these spreading out in the shape of a fan. In Kent, one Ash is reputed to be 146 feet high and about 12 feet in girth. As you know the Ash is very late in coming into leaf, and there is a superstition that should the leaves of this tree come before those of the Oak we are sure to have a wet summer.

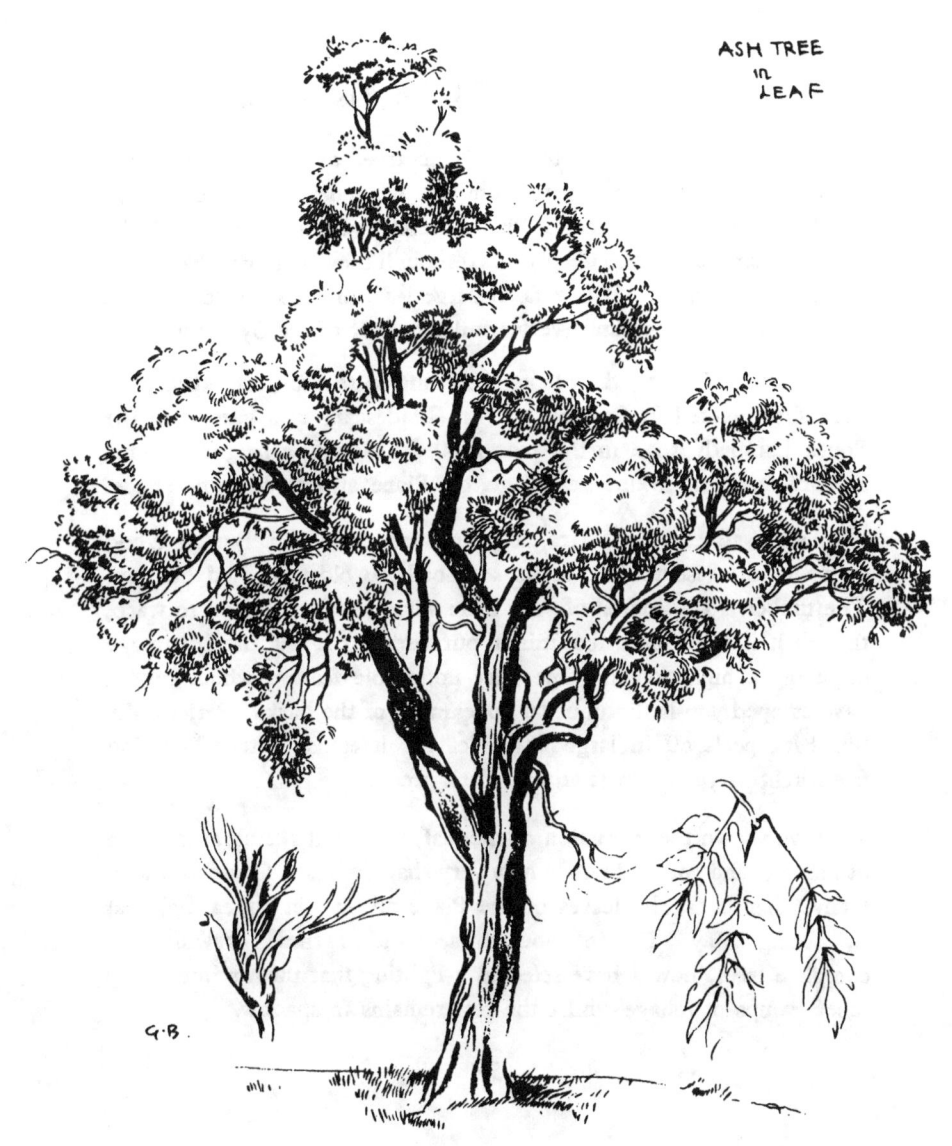

ASH TREE
in
LEAF

G·B·

PLATE 29. PLANE TREE IN FULL LEAF

There are two varieties of the Plane tree, the Oriental and the Occidental. They are very similar in general character, but the leaves of the Occidental Plane, which we might well call the London Plane, are not so deeply lobed though they are larger than those of the other variety. It is a fairly large leaf, divided into about five lobes, and is in appearance very similar to that of the Sycamore.

A native of Greece, the Plane, according to records, is said to have been first planted in London by Mr. Tradescant in a garden in the South Lambeth Road in the year 1640. Reaching a height of some seventy feet with luxuriant foliage, the Plane affords welcome shade.

In some states of America, it is referred to as the Button-Wood owing to the resemblance of its seed-balls to old-fashioned buttons. The timber is considered of very little value as it is inclined to warp, though it is used for a few minor purposes for it has the advantage of taking a high polish. One very noticeable feature which cannot have escaped you is the unusual appearance of the bark. Periodically this bark peels off in large flakes leaving irregular patches ranging from lightish yellow to fawn and dark green.

I have shown the formation of the leaf in a small sketch at the side of the tree, and you will notice how very shapely it is. Compared with many other trees, the leaves of the Plane are late in appearing, that is, during May. I want you to see, in all these drawings of complete trees, how I have selected a lighting that throws into sharp relief groups of foliage whilst the rest remains in shadow.

PLANE TREE
ⁱ FULL LEAF

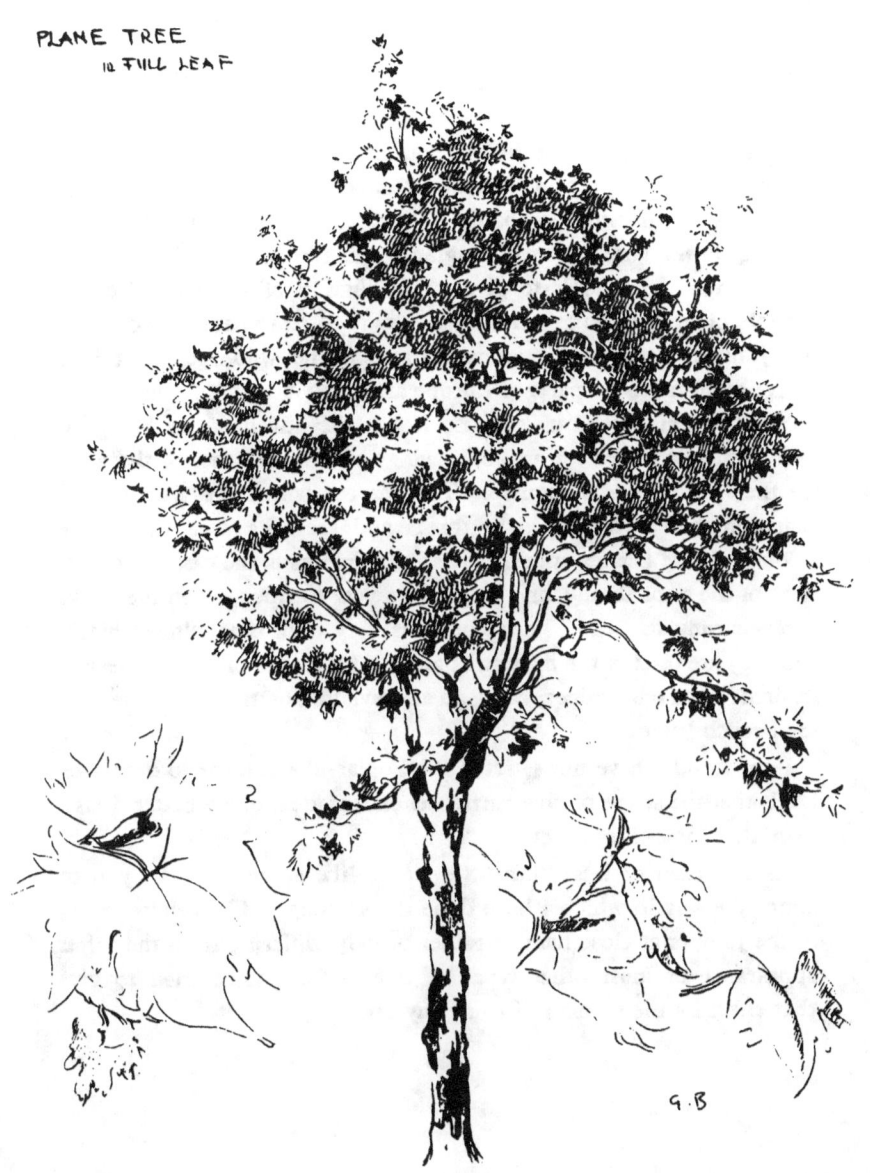

G·B

PLATE 30. JUNIPER

To see the Juniper in profusion, you must go to the North Downs of Surrey where one portion is named Juniper Hill. Often in shape it resembles a miniature Lombardy Poplar, and is very shapely indeed. On the downs and heaths of England, the Juniper is so often quite small that it is difficult to give it the dignity of the term " tree " though, of course, the prophet Elijah was reputed to have rested under the Juniper Tree on his journey through the wilderness. It is a native of all northern parts of Europe and in Britain it is found largely on chalky soil. For our purpose it has the advantage of being an evergreen so that we can make drawings of it at all times of the year, weather permitting of course. The leaves, which are narrow and sharp-pointed are arranged in threes and are of a dark rich green colour. Little berries appear instead of cones as is the case with most trees of the same family, and they take a year to ripen, when they have a very strong flavour. Their colour is very dark blue, almost black, and they are used in the making of gin. As a matter of fact gin derives its name from the Juniper, being an abbreviation of the word *genévrier*, the French Juniper.

I am afraid I have not selected the Poplar-like Juniper to draw, for I felt that the shape of this particular one, made a much better design than the flame-like variety.

As this tree, or bush, has little leaves like spines, I want you to notice the way in which I have done the shading. The general effect of the Juniper at close hand is rather prickly, differing from the softer appearance of most other types of trees. So I have tried to give that effect by the manner of using my line.

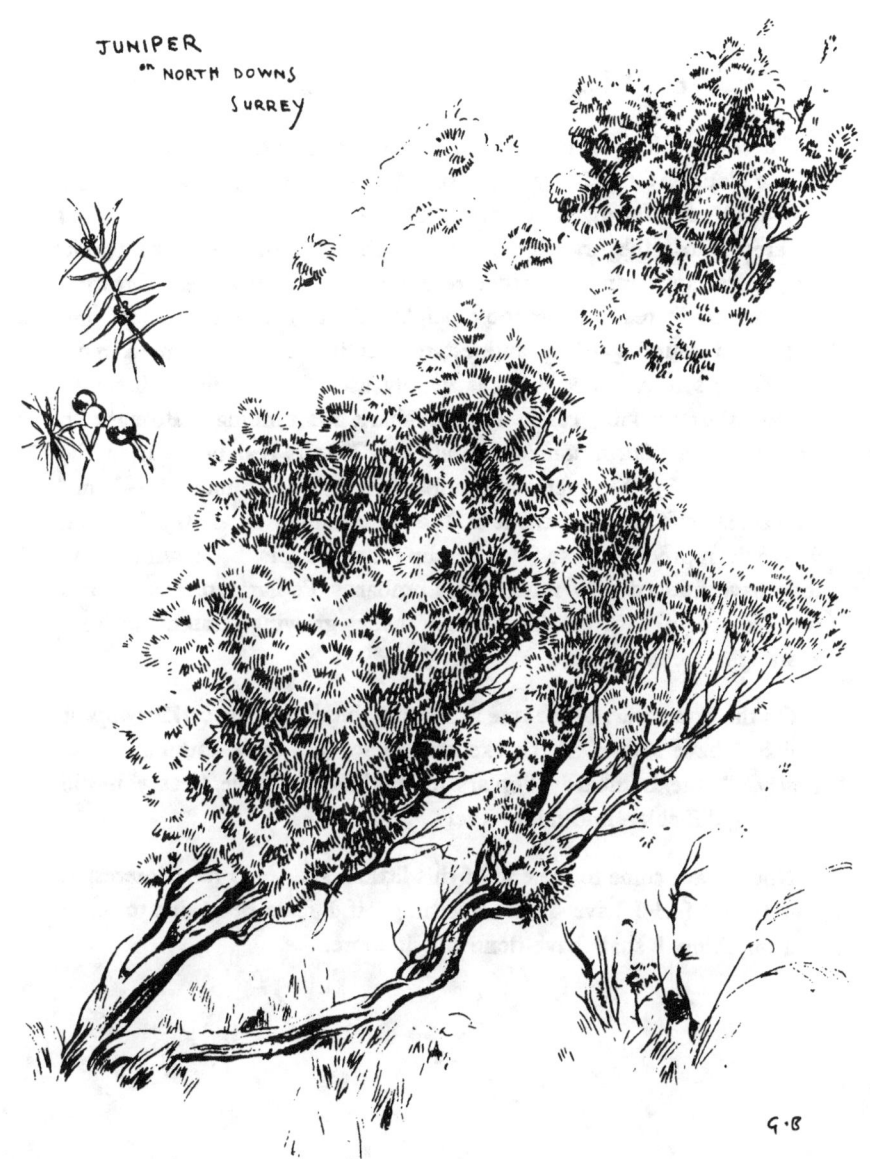

JUNIPER
on NORTH DOWNS
SURREY

G·B

PLATE 31. LOMBARDY POPLAR

There are three main species of Poplar found in England, the White Poplar, Grey Poplar and the Aspen. The Lombardy Poplar shown in my drawing, is a variety of Black Poplar with the marked difference that the branches grow straight upwards from the trunk. In general appearance it rather resembles a church spire. Growing very rapidly, it reaches the noble height of over one hundred feet, and if planted round gardens and estates, as it often is, forms a most decorative screen. The wood is mainly used for making such things as boxes or packing cases, and the bark for tanning. Brought to England from Turin somewhere about 1758, its real home is in the Himalayas. By the rivers of Lombardy it grows abundantly—hence its name,—and in England it is the best known of all the Poplars, where it reproduces itself by sending up suckers. In winter you may have noticed how much the Lombardy Poplar reminds us of a witches broom with all those fine branches growing straight up from a straight stem.

On the upper part of the tree in March, those jolly red catkins appear which I have shown in the sketch. They are male catkins and as nearly all the Lombardy Poplars in England are male trees you will have no difficulty in finding them.

Now I have come to the end of this little book. If I have interested you I shall feel I have done something; if I have been able to teach you anything I shall have done much more.

GREGORY
BROWN

LOMBARDY
POPLAR

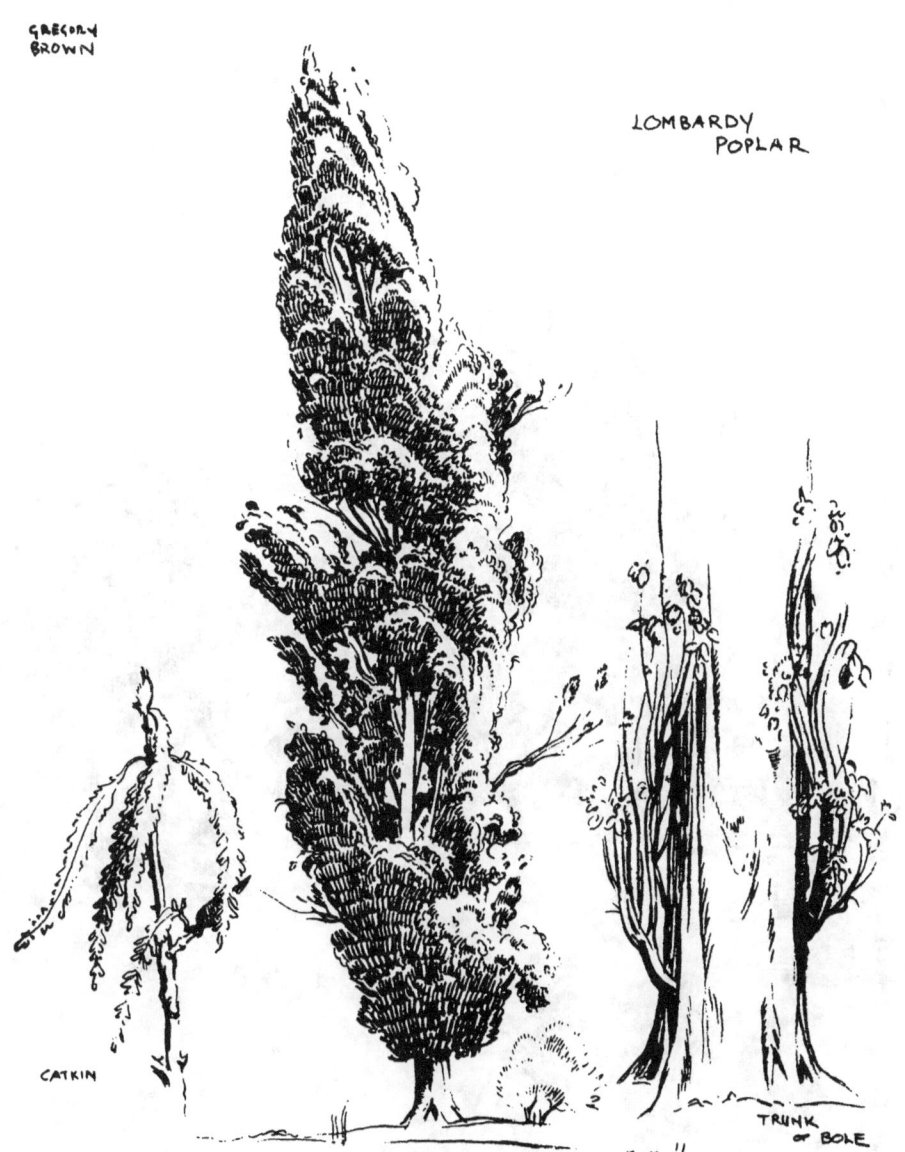

CATKIN

TRUNK
or BOLE

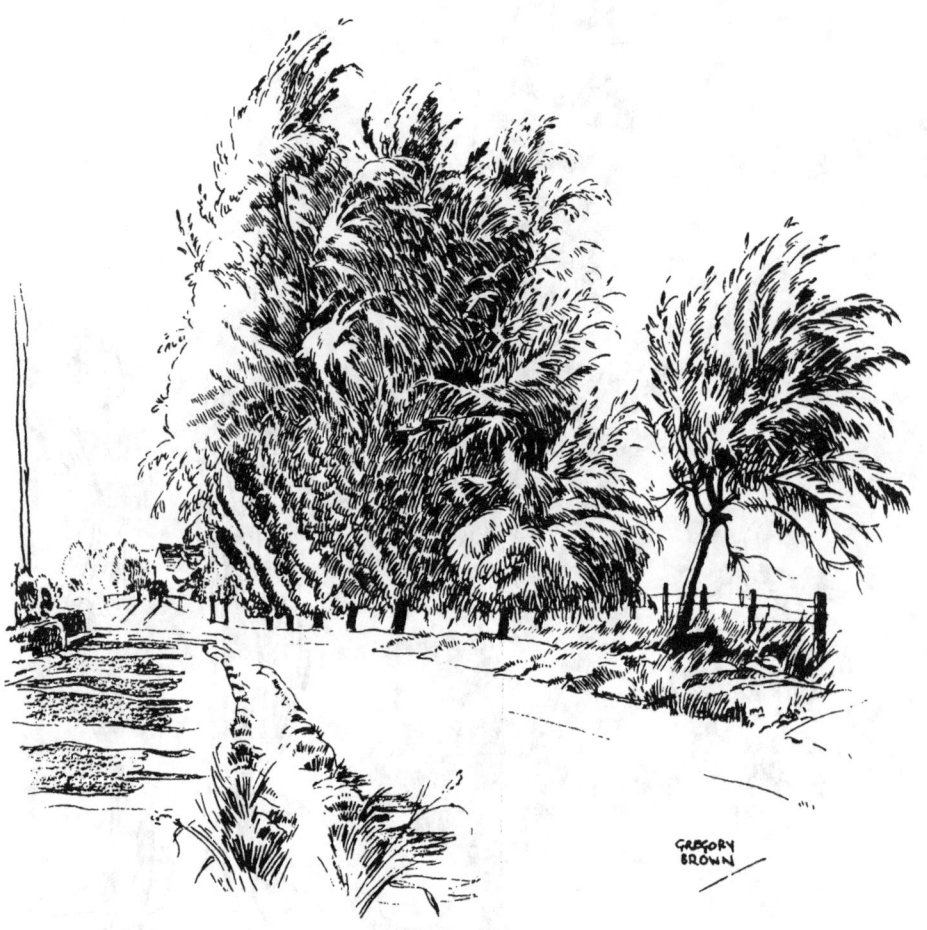

WILLOWS
IN THE WIND
BROCKHAM LANE
SURREY

GREGORY
BROWN

COACHWHIP PUBLICATIONS

COACHWHIPBOOKS.COM

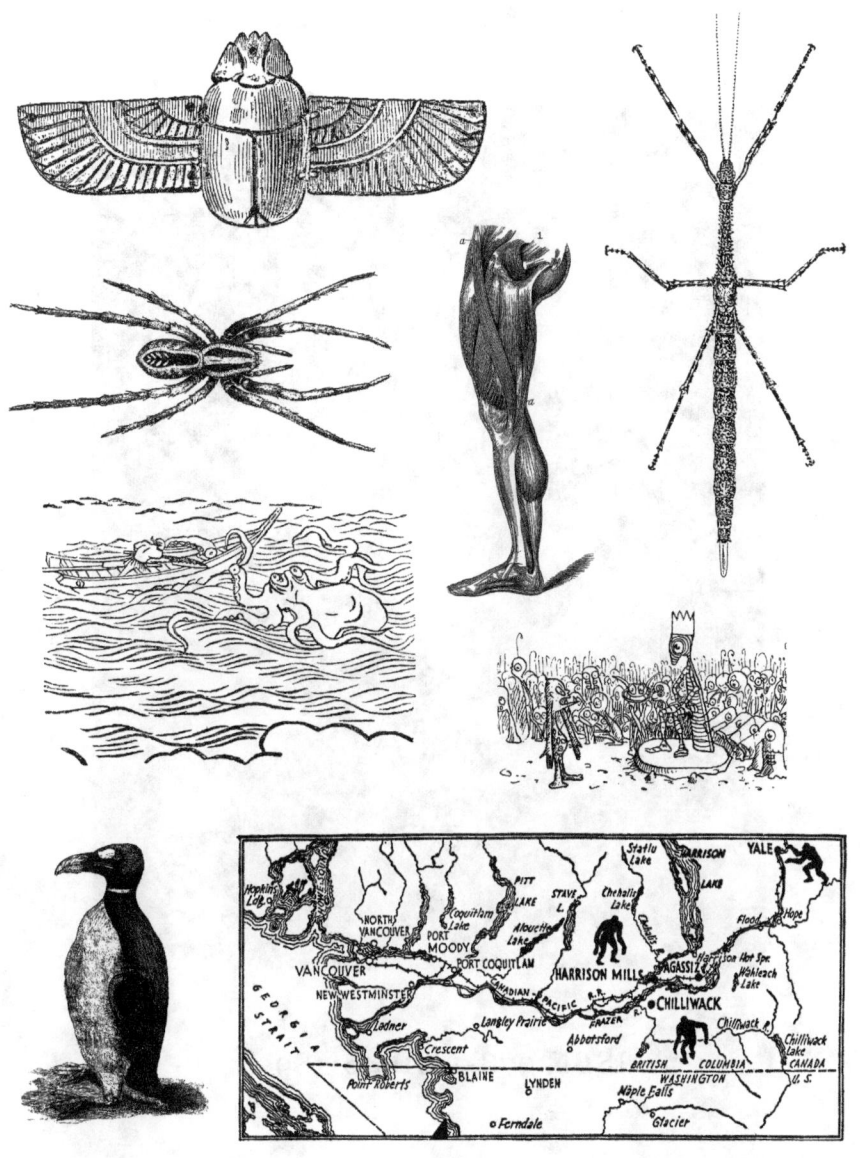

Coachwhip Publications

CoachwhipBooks.com

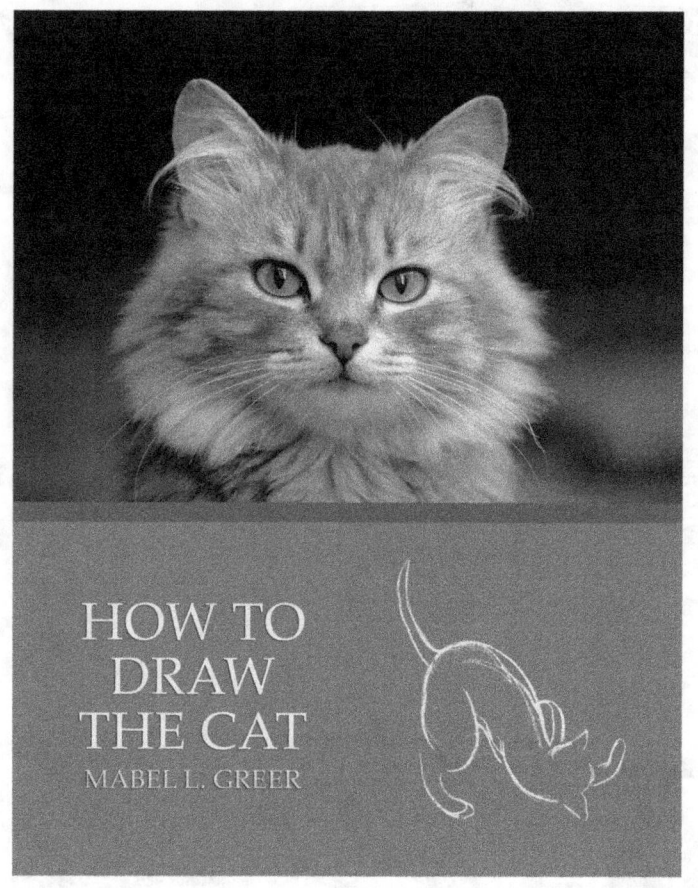

HOW TO
DRAW
THE CAT
MABEL L. GREER

ISBN 978-1-61646-189-8

COACHWHIP PUBLICATIONS

COACHWHIPBOOKS.COM

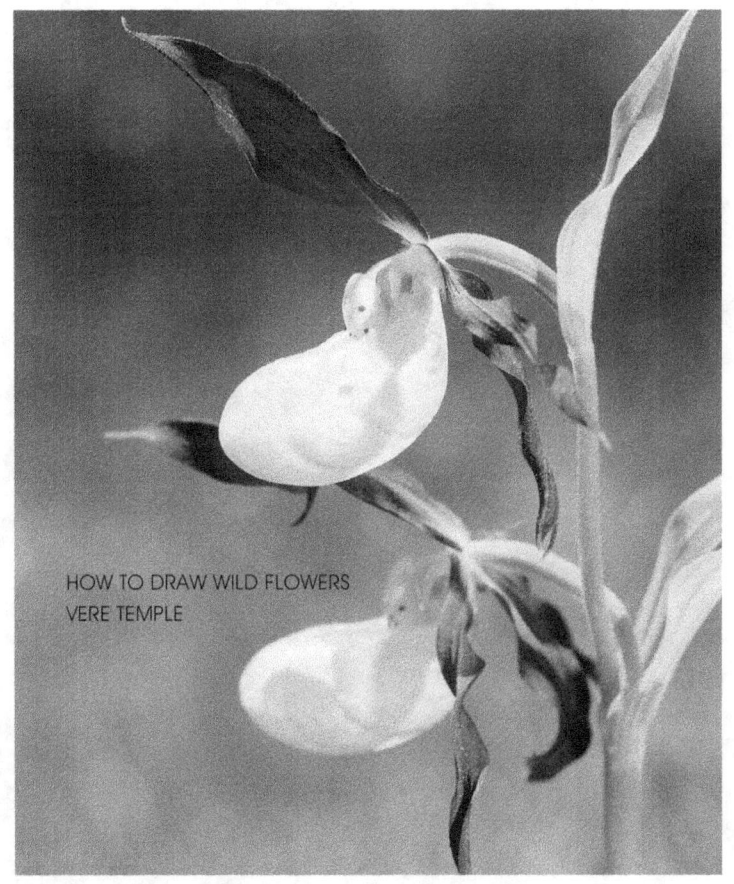

HOW TO DRAW WILD FLOWERS
VERE TEMPLE

ISBN 978-1-61646-196-6

www.ingramcontent.com/pod-product-compliance
Lightning Source LLC
Chambersburg PA
CBHW081304170526
45165CB00011B/3404